Where There's a Will, There's a Way!

A Guide to Wills, Living Trusts, Taxes

and Planning for the Ones You Love

Second Edition

by Madeline Gauthier, Attorney at Law
LL.M. Taxation

Copyright © 2007 by Madeline Gauthier

First Edition 2002
Second Edition 2007

This publication is designed to provide accurate and authoritative information in regard to the subject matter covered. It is sold with the understanding that the publisher is not engaged in rendering legal, accounting or other professional service. If legal advice or other expert assistance is required, the services of a competent professional person should be sought. (From a Declaration of Principles jointly adopted by a Committee of the American Bar Association and a Committee of Publishers and Associations.)

To ensure compliance with requirements imposed by the U.S. Internal Revenue Service, we inform you that any tax advice contained in this communication was not intended or written to be used, and cannot be used, by any taxpayer, for the purpose of avoiding tax-related penalties under the U.S. Internal Revenue Code. You should seek advice from an independent tax advisor regarding your personal circumstances.

For additional copies, please order from the web site
madelinegauthier.com

or contact:

Madeline Gauthier, Bellevue, WA
Phone: 425-637-3019 ex 3010
E-mail for ordering:
willsbookwashington@msn.com

Table of Contents

Introduction

It's an amazing fact: 70% of Americans (lawyers included) have not written a Last Will or Living Trust. The most common reason couples give is that they could not agree on the details, especially who should be the guardians of their children. Many people avoid preparing written instructions because it is so painful to think about their own demise. They fail to realize that if they do not come to some decision, then the courts will decide for them!

Deciding on the details of a Will or Living Trust is hard work for the clients. They have to become active in planning for the time when they are gone. Its an emotional task, but one that saves the remaining family members a lot of work, if it's done well. I always cover three main topics with my clients when they want a Will or a Living Trust:

1. Are there tax consequences if you, or you and your partner together, pass on? Are there things you could do during life that would lessen the tax burden at death? This is not the most important topic, but it is the one people usually need to cover first, to fully grasp their situation. Tax considerations give us only one perspective on the assets.

2. Caring for the people you love is the most important topic on the agenda. So the most important question is: what should happen for your loved ones when you pass on? This includes plans for your children, your parents who may survive you into their old age, other relatives who may need help through life disabilities, and charities you wish to remember.

3. The other topic concerns your wishes for care during a time of your own disability in life, final care, choices

about continuing life support if terminally ill (including if you are pregnant and near death), and final services.

Throughout this book, I talk about using techniques that legally avoid the gift and estate tax. You need to have a general understanding of general tax policy. It is driven by two goals: One is to raise money for the treasury. The other is to motivate people to act in ways that benefit the public. For instance, home ownership produces stable neighborhoods, a tax base for schools, local interest in improvements, etc. So, the government allows a tax deduction for the interest you pay on your home loan. Charities and non-profit organizations provice public services like hospital care for those without adequate funds of their own, education for disabled persons, foster care for homeless children, and public art projects. When you give money to those organizations, it allows them to provide these services and the government doesn't have to take on the responsibilities. You get a tax deduction as encouragement to make the donation.

But the most important thing I want to tell you is that "where there's a Will there's a way". In other words, if you put your wishes in a Will or Living Trust, the result will be better than if you let the state choose your final gifts and make the plans for your loved ones. Equally important, you need competent professional help to get this done. Please remember that this is not a "do it yourself" book. It is designed to give you ideas that you can discuss with your own attorney.

I hope the thoughts here are helpful to you.

Part One - Basic Estate Planning

Chapter 1: The Basic Will

Everybody has a Will. That's because the State Legislature where you live wrote one for you! Maybe you like what the legislature wrote. Maybe not. Most of us don't like it. The main reason that I don't like my state's Will is that it gives money to children when they turn 18. Maybe you were a wise genius at 18. I was not, and I'm not sure that I am even now! The state's Will allows 18 year olds to receive their inheritance; you can write your Will and make your youngsters wait awhile! The State's Will won't give money to charities. It might provide for your parents, but maybe not. The State has to presume that you didn't trust anyone to handle your affairs without being supervised, because if you had trusted someone, you would have told us. That means the Courts will supervise every move that your Administrator makes. The Personal Representative (also called an Executor or an Administrator) can't sell the house without the Court reviewing all the offers. She can't clean out your home or have a garage sale without an order from the Court. I make much more money on probate cases when there is no Will or Living Trust, so I shouldn't complain. But it doesn't make much sense, does it? A decent Will, even with tax planning, costs less than the first appearance at Court when I have to present a probate case without a Will.

A decent Will isn't hard to produce, but it takes some time to figure out what's important to you. (This doesn't mean you should get a form at the stationery store and fill in the blanks!) There are really only two questions you need to answer, before we can produce a Last Will that truly reflects your last wishes.

First: Who do you love and how should they be taken care of after you are gone?

3

Second: Is there any tax planning that should be done if you die, or you and your spouse die at nearly the same time?

So who do you love? The usual answer is "my spouse", "my partner", "my kids". I expect those answers. Now think of your larger family. Maybe you've got an elder on your list of special people, or a disabled sister or brother. Do they need special school or have unusual talents that should be nurtured? Will your aging parents need additional income if inflation outpaces their pensions? So, again, who do you love? And what do you want to do for them? Once you have identified those people, or charities, then the planning can begin.

You may love someone, but that doesn't mean they get cash. Some people are too young, too old, too dedicated to drinking, too involved with an abuser or too nonchalant to handle money all by themselves. I'm not convinced that withholding an inheritance should be a way to punish someone you otherwise love. When a client says, "I'd like to leave money to all my sisters, but not to my brother, because he drinks and he can't handle it," my response is this: "Tell me more about your brother? Is the problem that he squanders money? Then maybe you should leave the money to go into a trust, and let the trustee give him an allowance every month. Maybe we should write the Will, telling your Personal Representative to buy an annuity from your life insurance agent and that will give him a reliable income for life. If the problem is that he isn't good to his family, then maybe we should put aside the money that would have been his share, and create an education trust for his kids. The real question is this: do you need to leave him out entirely, or do you love him enough to leave money in a way that meets his needs or helps his family? Or will that kind of plan add to his problems by not making him responsible?"

Most of my clients want to take care of spouses and their own kids, plus their parents if they need help. The next question is harder: if all of those people were gone, then what should happen to your money? If everything they've acquired is joint, I encourage couples to give half to each side of the family. If there are some assets that were earned before marriage or inherited, we divide it like this:

> "If neither my spouse nor my children or grandchildren survive me, I leave all my property as follows:
>
> All of my separate property (including my inheritance from my father) and one half of my property owned with my spouse, to my surviving siblings or their surviving issue, in equal shares
>
> One half of my property owned with my spouse, to my spouse's surviving siblings or their surviving issue, in equal shares"

Sometimes clients insist that they want to leave their half of the assets to their own family and let their spouse do the same. But think this through. If the husband dies first, and the wife, being in the same ugly accident, dies five months later, then she has inherited everything. Her Will says to leave what she has only to her family, and his family doesn't get any share of what he earned. It's a windfall to her family. Honestly, can't you envision the feelings of being cheated that are going to go on in such a case? Can't you see his family saying something ugly about what just happened? And can you blame them? We're just human. Our feelings are real and have to be acknowledged. When I go, I want all the people who loved me to comfort each other and to share their memories. I don't want them refusing to see each other at Christmas, and missing the cousins' weddings. The best way to do this is to honor all the people who loved a couple, make sure they are all included. I know this type of sharing between the two families isn't realistic if the husband dies, the wife survives 10 years and hasn't kept up a relationship with that family. By then, everyone expects that she'll have a new plan, primarily for her own family. But for the short term, considering accidents, it's a good plan.

One of the loveliest families I met involved a couple who were not married. The man and woman had lived together for about seven years, but there is no common law marriage in this state. They bought a beautiful home together. She loved his mother. They always laughed about how they should really get married, but they just never got around to it. He died in an accident, leaving no Will. I wished that she wasn't in that situation. But in leaving, she inherited the gift of his family, who treasured her as though she were a daughter. His mother and his brother were her best advocates. They loved her and they wanted to treat her the way they would have treated a legal wife. They wanted her to have everything and were willing to do whatever was necessary to make that happen. You are probably thinking that the easy way out was to let the mother and the brother inherit his assets and then have them transfer it to the woman. You are right, but that would have created gift tax problems for them. We had another way out. She filed a claim for his half of the property, saying that they'd made a contract to leave everything to each other. The mother and the son didn't oppose it, and they signed an agreement saying that she should receive everything from the estate. It might have been ugly. The saving grace was a fabulous family.

Here is a list of things to ask yourself as you prepare to write a Will or Living Trust:

- Who do you love?
- Do any of those people have special problems that we should plan for?
- How should your money be used to help them rise to their highest potential, or meet their needs?
- What should we do to be sure they'll be kind to one another when you are gone (as opposed to fighting over your money)?

Chapter 2: Selecting the Guardians

Of all the reasons people give me for not getting their Wills done, naming a guardian for the children is the most common. And oddly, getting on an airplane for a trip is the most commonly given reason for getting Wills done, because the parents realize they may die and they haven't named guardians yet (although they are at more risk being in their cars going to work each day!). That's why the holiday season is my busiest time of the work year.

It is no small task to name guardians. Let's be honest. There is no one who would raise your children the way you would do it. These children were given to you and you are specially prepared to do this job. But we are not the Giver of Life. We don't get to decide everything. So who would do the best job in raising your kids if you and your spouse couldn't do it? And if those people aren't available, then who is your second choice? Keep in mind that your selected guardians may not be able to serve (they've gotten older), or they may be in the same terrible accident that you die in.

There are no magic answers and there are no words of wisdom that I can share. I've only got guidelines:

- Who shares your same temperament?
- Who is at an age where they could raise these kids through high school?
- Who has a stable home?
- Who can adjust to having a new family move in
- Who can offer your children comfort when they are in crisis after your death?
- Who has a religion that you share, or at best, that your kids can tolerate (if they have all the other attributes you are looking for but are of a different faith)?

You aren't looking for the people with the most money or the most education. You are looking for someone to nurture your children to be the best adults that their gene pool will allow. Its not easy.

Chapter 3: **Trusts for your Children and Others**

Trusts as a part of your Will

Early in my career, I thought that twenty-one was a fine age to distribute money to children. I always tell the story of the day my daughter came to visit on her 21st birthday. She was very proud of the new boots she had just bought. I asked her how much they cost, as I took a sip of my tea. I choked and coughed when she told me that they cost as much as I spent on food for me and her sister in a month! I bit my tongue, because she was 21, but I mumbled to myself that I was not going to give her a dime until she was much older. (To her credit, she still has the boots after ten years. They were a good buy).

Time Magazine ran an article called "Secrets of The Teen Brain".[1] It talked about the latest research on brain development from birth to adulthood. What I've been instinctively saying for years is now scientifically proven: the brain isn't fully developed until age twenty-five. If Hertz won't rent them a car, you shouldn't give them money. When I say this to people who are just barely twenty-five and earning a living, I have to remind them that earned money and inherited money are not the same. Inherited money feels like Monopoly money. Earned money involves unpleasant bosses, overtime, responding to performance reviews, union negotiations and sleepless nights.

Anybody under twenty-five should not inherit money outright; instead, it should be kept in a trust. It won't cost you a fortune and yes, you need one, even if you aren't "rich" ("rich" is a concept that is relative). You can have a family member serve as the trustee. The trustee can give money to the kids, or to someone else for the kids, using the guidelines you've set out in the trust. They can have enough

---

[1]Time Magazine, May 10, 2004.

9

money to get through school and maybe even to put a down payment on a home. I guess they could eventually squander it. But make them wait awhile. Who knows? Your daughter's first husband, at 22, may be one of those guys who thinks he knows everything, and she may let him invest her money right down the toilet. Or maybe they get a divorce when she's 25, and by then she's put all the money into a jointly owned house with him. Say good-bye to that money!

A trust is a way to leave the money for someone else's care, and still keep control for awhile. A trust is an "artificial person", and like all persons, it has a tax identification number. It must file a tax return. This artificial person has its marching orders! It is told what it can and can't pay for, using the trust document you prepared. And those directions are carried out by a trustee. You can have a trust in your Last Will or in a Living Will, both of which tell us how to give money to your loved ones when you are gone. These take effect after your death so you might hear them referred to as "testamentary trusts". You could also create a trust that has money and starts operating while you are still alive. You might hear these referred to as "intervivos trusts".

You can put directions you want into the trust document. I personally go for lots of education, because nobody can take away what's inside your head. Ditto for educational experiences (for instance, a trip with the church to build homes in Mexico). I also like giving a modest down payment on a first home (5% down and 5% for closing costs), or money for a bigger home if there are small children.

Let's not forget about the things your guardian will need. If they've taken in more children, get them a housekeeper. I'm also a fan of making sure the relatives have enough money to come and visit your children if they don't live near your kids. If the guardians need a bigger house, be sure the trustee can loan them the extra they need, interest free, for the time that your kids are living with them. They can pay back the loan when the kids no longer live there.

Your money is supposed to help make your kids's life go smoothly if you are gone. It's not supposed to be hoarded for the time when the kids are older. It's definitely supposed to provide for them, make it easy for the guardians to raise them, give them an education, and maybe have some money for other things, like a down payment on a home. We will never know in advance what's just right for our kids, so if I have to accept some possibility of error, I tend to err on the side of generous education and delayed outright distribution. Be a realist. Ask yourself this question: if somebody gave me $50,000 today, what would I do with it? My own answer is scary! I bet you thought about a boat, a vacation, a face lift, a timeshare, a new car (in almost every probate, the heir buys a new car). That money can go away in a heartbeat, even for you and me. Let's not tempt our kids. Let them grow up first. Really grow up.

You Can Create A Trust During Your Lifetime

Most of the discussion about trusts in this book will center on trusts that are created as a part of your Last Will or Living Trust. The truth is that sometimes people create trusts during their lifetimes. They have the excess assets, they want to distribute them now for tax planning that is advantageous. The next few pages are a sampling of ways to help your family accept the transfer of assets, without giving them control before either of you are ready for it.

The Crummey Trust

The Crummey Trust sounds like something the children might say: "They set up the trust for me, and I can't have any of the money until they die. It is a crummy deal!" they complain. Many a prudent parent has concerns about what the children might do with instant

11

cash. Particularly if the children are young, it may destroy their personal initiative and commitment to hard work.[2]

This planning tool is actually named after a well known tax case, in which the father wanted to move money out of his accounts and over to his children. Instead of giving them cash to spend during his lifetime, he created a trust. He gave the trustee $10,000 for the benefit of each child. The children had the right to withdraw the money for a period of 30 days after the trustee sent them notice. If the child didn't take the money, then it stayed in the trust account permanently, or until the trustee might decide to distribute it during the father's life. After the father died, the money would be distributed on a schedule. The benefit to both father and children was that at the time of his death, Mr. Crummey would not own the money. The trust owned it. It would not be included in his taxable estate.

The IRS argued that the father did not make a tax-free gift. The IRS said the gifts were taxable to the father, because the children never had an immediate right to the funds.[3] The court ruled that the IRS was incorrect. For up to 30 days, the children could take the money outright. The fact that the children didn't take the money out and that the money then remained in the trust (the children could never ask for it later) was beside the point.

---

[2] For a good discussion of the effects of gifting money to children, read *The Millionaire Next Door* by Thomas Stanley and William Danko, Longstreet Press, Inc., 1996). You might also like the DVD "Born Rich", a documentary film about the challenges faced by children of privilege.

[3] The rules on tax free gifting are better described in Chapter 10. Generally, in order to have a tax free gift, the money must be a "completed gift", meaning that the receiver of the gift has an immediate access to it, with no requirements.

The Crummey Trust is a great way to transfer money to younger members of the family, without actually letting them have control. This trust works whether the children are 4 years old or 45!

There are some traps in arranging this trust:

- You must have a period of time, no less than 30 days, in which the beneficiaries may choose to withdraw the funds. (Don't offer it to them on December 15.)

- If they do ask for the funds at that time, the trustee must distribute the money to them, with no questions asked.

- If the IRS thinks that the parent has threatened or cajoled a child to decline the money, then the gift isn't completed. Don't do it!

Parents handle this best by appealing to the sensibilities of the youngster, who can understand that money that leaves the parent's account is not taxed. The children benefit by getting more money, untaxed, when the parent dies. They should want to encourage Dad to increase their inheritance this way and the parents can remind the children that they can show their maturity by not withdrawing the funds. But let's face it: some kids are going to be kids, so they will be immature for a long while! They'll demand their money now. So an alternate solution for parents is to put most of the funds into the trust before the children turn 18 years old. The guardian makes the decision to decline taking the funds.

Irrevocable Life Insurance Trust

There is a variation to this theme often called the Irrevocable Life Insurance Trust (ILIT). Like the Crummey Trust, it is legal and provides a way to transfer money to the heirs.

Here's how it works: The parent puts money into the trust. Assuming the children decide not to draw the funds out, the trustee has funds to invest. Banking, opening a brokerage account, buying real estate - there are many choices. One thing the trustee can do is buy life insurance covering the life of the parent. Many use the *Second to Die* type of policy that pays the proceeds upon the death of the second parent. This choice may maximize the investment.

The good news is that the insurance proceeds won't ever be included in the parent's taxable estate, because the parent didn't buy the life insurance. The trust bought it. The IRS cannot tax this money. The bad news is that a child might decide to take the funds at the time of the contribution rather than let the funds remain in the trust. If there is an insurance premium due and the children demand the money, the whole plan may collapse.

Parents facing this dilemma have a few choices. One is to pay all the premiums before the children turn 18. Another is to arrange for the insurance premiums to be small enough payments so that if one child won't go along with the program, at least there is enough money going into the trust for the other children that the trustee can still make the payments.

Here's an example, using the Crummey Trust and the ILIT:

> Parents created a Crummey Trust, hoping that the trustee would purchase life insurance. They made a preliminary application for the life insurance, but didn't commit to it or pay for it. The insurance premium for a $1 million life insurance policy for the parents was $40,000 in a lump sum, or $4,500 per year for 10 years. They had three children. The parents decided they wanted to pay the premiums over 10 years. Their oldest child was 11 when they started the program. When she got to be 17, the little darling turned into a

parent-hating defiant monster. She wanted to move out and demanded that they support that bad habit. They had a sinking feeling that if they funded the trust the next few years, she'd demand her money. They had four years left on the contract, at $4,500. If she demanded her share, not only would she be out of the nest on their ticket; the wouldn't have sufficient funds to pay the insurance premium. So in the year she was 17, they made a payment of $18,000 to the trust. That was a tax free gift, because it was less than the yearly exclusionary amount for all three children. The insurance contract was fully paid before she turned 18, and no more payments were made until she blossomed into the genteel young woman they knew she'd become. They eventually put more money into the trust, beyond what the insurance contract required.

College Savings Plans

This chapter wouldn't be complete without a discussion of college savings plans under IRS Code 529. Here's how it works:

You want the grandchild to go to college, so you want to fund that project. The money goes into an approved plan; it grows tax-free until it is time for college. If it is used for education expenses, it is not taxed when withdrawn. School expenses include tuition, books, supplies, room and board, and required fees.

Under the normal gift tax rules, you can currently give up to $12,000 per year to anyone[4]. If you wanted to give away $24,000 today to one person, and have it count for this year and next year, you

---

[4]Remember, this number goes up with inflation. See Chapter 10 for a full explanation.

normally wouldn't be able to do so, without attracting a gift tax. But you can make a gift for this year, and for years into the future, right now, if you are gifting into an IRA Code 529 plan! With the 529 plan, you can gift the money for five years into the future! If you really want to commit to the project, you can make five years of gifts, for you and for your spouse, all at once, for the same beneficiary. The value of gifting five year's worth of contributions all at once is that the money is earning tax free income for the next five years.

You can change the name of the beneficiary if you need to. Suppose you create a 529 plan for your niece and later she doesn't want to go to college. You can change the plan to be used for her brother. Or you can just change your mind, and take the money back, although there will be some tax and penalties if you do. You can contribute up to $250,000 to a 529 plan for any person.

The benefits of the 529 plan are outstanding. The money is removed from your estate, but you still have some control over who is getting the money. It is growing tax-free in a safe environment and you can change your mind. Is there anything else you could ask for? Okay, good grades and full attendance for your youngster are on the list, but as far as the tax and gifting benefits go, this transfer is a fabulous deal.

Many states have 529 plans approved by the IRS. Some states, like Washington, have pre-paid tuition plans, so you are paying today's price for tuition credits, and your youngster can use them in the future, no matter if the price for tuition went up. The plan can be transferred to another state. Other states have investment programs, allowing you to put money into the stock market for investment. You can buy any state's 529 plan, no matter where you live. Talk to your state's representative or to a stock broker about this. You'll be impressed with this particular tax code provision.

Remember that the goals of the tax code are to raise money and to encourage people to behave in socially acceptable ways. Paying for someone's education is socially acceptable. The only down side is that if the person doesn't want to go to college, and you have no one else to give the money to, you'll have to take it back. The penalty is usually 10%, and you'll owe income tax on the gain in the account. But you've still had the money growing tax-free for years.

The Uniform Transfers to Minors Act

You may be thinking that trusts are too much work and since you don't have a taxable estate anyway, there is no need to go to the bother and expense to create the trust. When the grandparents send money gifts, you just deposit it into the bank (using the **Uniform Transfers to Minors Act** or whatever law your state has to prevent children from taking money). Then when the youngster is ready for college, the money will be there.

The plan should work fine if:

1. Junior decides to get some advanced education when he is out of high school.

2. Junior has no interest in buying a car.

3. Junior is generally emotionally healthy and has some plans for himself.

Youth being what it is, you cannot count on your smart six year old to behave sensibly at age 21. If you are depositing gifts into a bank or brokerage account under the Uniform Transfers to Minors

Act, the child can take the money at age 21.[5] My practice has revealed too many stories of disaster in this area, so I urge you to consider setting up a trust or 529 plan for your youngsters, even if you don't have a taxable estate.

Trusts for Relatives

Most people tell me that they want to leave all their money to their children (or the children's trustee) if their spouse doesn't survive. That's the usual order of things. But sometimes deaths don't happen in the usual order. An *out of order death* is a situation when the child dies first, leaving his/her parents behind.

Every parent wants to leave money to provide for their minor children to be raised. Consider this: the parents pass away, and their home, insurance, retirement and other assets are liquidated. Suppose they leave $1 million to care for the children. That will be invested and generate about $40,000 per year. In addition, the guardian will receive Social Security payments because the parents are gone. In that scenario, there will be more than enough money for the children. We need to ask if there are other relatives who need to be provided for.

It makes sense to consider the total of all the needs you would like to meet if you were still here. Ask yourself the question: Is there anyone who would need support from me if I were to live a long and natural life? Most often, the initial answer is "no". What about your parents? Are they financially secure, or do you think you might help them during their later years? Are all your brothers and sisters healthy and able to support themselves?

---

[5]Washington law has recently created an opportunity for the gift to be held until the individual attains age 25. See Revised Code of Washington, 11.114.200, effective July 1, 2007.

Once I have asked the questions above, the answer changes about half the time. Yes, it is likely that inflation will outpace Mother's retirement and savings in the coming years. You fully expect that if Mom needed a new roof or if her car needed repair, you'd write the check in an instant. You would help your sister who is disabled and living on a small disability check. And if any of those things are true, it doesn't make sense to leave all of the money to the children's trust.

The children's trust has very specific directions to pay only for your children. There is no authority in the children's trust to direct money over to Mom or your sister. Here is a solution to the problem: if you have someone who needs additional care (such as a parent) carve out an amount (maybe 10% or 20%) that would otherwise have gone to the kids, and leave it in a trust for the relative's lifetime.[6] At the end of that person's life, whatever is left goes back into the children's trust. There are choices to be made about how to structure the trust. For instance, some people want the trust to give out all the income but none of the principal. Others want the trust to pay only for the extra expenses that Medicaid doesn't cover. Others don't want to limit the trust distributions at all; but if there is any money left in the trust, they definitely want it to go to their children. Whatever you choose, they will be grateful.

Here is a summary of the things you should think about:

Anybody under 25 years old probably shouldn't inherit much money outright.

---

[6]See Chapters 4 and 8, for a greater discussion about caring for elders and disabled people who may need long term nursing care. In that situation, a trust is better than an outright gift.

- You can create a trust when you die, either in your Last Will or Living Trust, or you can do it during your life

- You can fund the trust with yearly payments

- Your trustee can use the trust funds to buy life insurance and it will never be taxable to your estate (if estate taxes are an issue)

- College Savings Plans allow you to save tax free for the youngster's education

- Gifts outside of a trust will have to be given to the children when they turn 18

- Don't forget to take care of your elders!

Chapter 4: Special Needs Trusts

Probably the hardest thing for parents is the worry that comes with planning for a disabled child. Although I've written generally about trusts for children in an earlier chapter, there is more planning that is needed for a child who has disabilities. Every year someone comes to me wanting to plan for a child who has autism, has a low IQ, suffers from psychosis, or has a head injury. Every parent that I've met with a special child is working very hard to give their child the best life has to offer. But they and I know that they will only live so long. Their child will have to be cared for after they are gone.

Sometimes I see the brothers and sisters of the disabled child, after the parents are gone. They come to me as probate cases. If I tell you the things that went wrong, then you will appreciate why it is so important to plan.

The Head Injury

Millie had a son who just couldn't keep a job. She was in her 80's when she asked me to write her Will. The son was 50 years old. She didn't know exactly what was wrong. He had never married or had a girlfriend. He couldn't keep a job, because his temper would get in the way and he usually told his boss off within about 2 weeks of being hired. He was capable of reading but he didn't understand many things that everybody else took for granted. He couldn't keep track of bills or arrange any kind of a project. For instance, if you needed a fence, you would open the phone book, call several fence builders, arrange to have them come to the house during hours you could be there. You'd get several bids, compare them and then make a choice. Eventually, you would inspect the work and pay the bill if the work was done properly. Her son wouldn't even know where to begin with a simple project such as this.

All that Millie could say about his disability was that when he was 15, he hit his head in the concrete bottom while diving at the public swimming pool. He was never the same after that. He never left home. She never had him diagnosed and she always supported him. Millie had one other child, a daughter, who was a few years younger. She was truly devoted to her mother and her brother. She agreed with her mother that, after her mother was gone, she wanted her mother's money to be used to care for her brother.

There were several plans that we could have used. For reasons that were personal to her, Millie objected to using a trust. As an alternate plan, Millie's money was gifted to the daughter, during her life. By the time Millie passed away, all the money was in the sister's hands. Now the brother couldn't squander the money his mother had left for him. His sister had it in her hands. (This plan only works if the other children are trustworthy and willing to care for a sibling). The other advantage was that the brother would then qualify for Social Security Disability benefits whenever he applied. But Millie didn't want to apply for benefits during her life. That was a personal decision and I couldn't persuade her to do it sooner.

When Millie died, the daughter jumped right in to help. But there was more to do than you can image. First, her brother had no means of support. She took the money her mother left, and put it in a separate account, using it only for her brother's needs. But the money Millie left behind would only carry the brother for about 5 years. The sister had her own husband and children to care for. She was willing to give up her inheritance for her brother, but she didn't feel that she could take her own earnings away from her own family. She and her husband were in their late 50's with two children in college. As they approached retirement, they didn't feel it would be safe for this loose-tempered brother could move in with them. At the same time, she wasn't going to let her brother live on the street. The sister began the process of getting him Social Security Disability benefits. Many people are turned down the first time they apply for Social Security

Disability, and when her brother was turned down, she had to hire someone to help with the application. Millie had never gotten a doctor to record the history of her son's problems, so that made it even harder to convince Social Security that he really had been disabled for so long. They had to get physicians to diagnose him, adding to the cost. In the meantime, her brother had to get some kind of a job and keep it. She went through several jobs with him, before he understood that he had to have some money each month to pay rent. He didn't have the luxury of yelling at his boss and quitting. She helped him move into a mobile home. Every single thing required for daily living, the brother had to be nudged into learning.

The Social Security application was finally approved. He received a small amount every month to supplement his job. The sister managed the money and paid bills from the fund when there wasn't enough from her brother's resources. It took about two years to get all of this done. The sister was a jewel, working very hard to care for her brother's needs. Yet, she was in tears several times. And she was furious with both of her parents for not planning better. She felt that they should have prepared a trust, gotten their son onto the Social Security process in his early 20's, and that they should have insisted that he be self supporting in whatever way that he was able, even with his disabilities. I've seen the same emotional roller coaster with other siblings when this scenario presents itself. They feel guilty for being normal while the sibling is disabled. They are angry with parents who didn't plan better. And they are furious at both their parents and the disabled sibling, who hasn't worked and hasn't been pushed to find a useful place in the world. Then they roll around to guilt again: how can we be so angry at my brother who has so little to work with?

The solution lies with the parents, who should plan for the problems long before they pass on. Leaving this problem to the surviving children is a terrible legacy.

Mental Illness

Recently a young woman came to see me, with similar problems. Her parents had another child, and the description made me think he was psychotic. He thought he had a case worth millions against a major corporation. He was going to use the money he'd win in the lawsuit to save the world. He was famous in his own mind. Every day, he heard God telling him to stay on the path of saving humanity. Her parents were caring for him in their home, but nothing more was going on in the way of planning. Although the dad was a doctor, there had never been a medical diagnosis.

She didn't cry while she was in my office, but she was upset. She knew her parents wouldn't be alive forever. Her father was already retired. She didn't want her brother living on the street. No one was getting him the mental health treatment that he so obviously needed. And this was all going to fall in her lap one day. She had small children, a wonderful husband, a good job, a lovely home and a fine mind. Those were treasures that she didn't want to destroy, and she knew they might be destroyed if she had to care for her brother after her parents were gone. I told her that she needed to beg and plead with her parents to get this handled, and right away. I told her to resort to making them feel guilty if nothing else worked! If they didn't feel guilty and get moving, then she was going to feel guilty later, when she couldn't handle both her own family responsibilities and her brother's care. It wasn't just her brother's life that was at stake; it was hers.

Physical Disability

Once I had a probate case, for a deceased single woman with no Will. She had two brothers, and both parents were gone. One brother was financially fine and healthy in every way. One had serious problems. He'd had polio as a child, leaving him in a wheel

24

chair. But it wasn't the polio that got the better of him. It was his attitude about it. He simply gave up at a young age, and the parents didn't push him. He said he didn't think he could have a job, so he didn't. When I met him, he was about 40. He'd never had a job and he had no education. He'd dropped out of high school. Many of his teeth were missing. He lived on public funds in low income housing. After his sister died, we found out that she had been paying for his food, driving him around, and helping with extra bills for a long time. He counted on the money she spent on him to survive.

The good news was that she was a successful employee of a major company, with about $750,000 in assets. The bad news was that the brother had been living on welfare so long that he didn't have a clue how to handle money he inherited. He had nothing, so he decided to buy everything! The older brother convinced him that they should buy a small place for him to live. But the spending went on. I urged them to put the money into trust, or at least put the home into trust, so creditors couldn't get to it, but to no avail. By the time the probate ended, the younger brother had spent every dime that he'd been given, and he had charged about $50,000 on credit cards. I knew it wouldn't be long before he lost the new home to pay his debts. When we last met, the older brother was sick with grief because he'd spent about a year helping to create a new opportunity for his younger sibling. He'd done the work on the home by himself, remodeling it for a wheelchair. He put in the new windows, painted the home, and arranged a car that was equipped for a wheel chair driver. The sad news was that this brother couldn't save himself. The money he inherited didn't make his life better, because he wasn't able to manage it himself. If his sister had signed a Will with even the simplest trust, he'd have a home that was paid for and nobody could touch it. He'd still be able to get his disability money from Social Security because he wouldn't be able to access the trust.

Here is the perfect plan. First, make a Will or a Living Trust[7], and leave money for the disabled child to a trustee of a Special Needs Trust. It must be written with specific provisions that allow the child to take advantage of state or federal government benefits, despite having your trust resources available. If it isn't properly written, the state will require that the trust assets be consumed before state funds are applied.[8] Next, get the child diagnosed if it hasn't already been done. Apply for Social Security benefits if the child is disabled. Do everything possible to help this child perform at his/her optimum level, including working at even the lowliest job. I say this last part whether your children are disabled or not. If your kids think they can rely on what you've got stowed away, they will not likely be motivated to be their best.

None of those things seem unusual, do they? Yet I see people every year who tell me that their parents didn't plan.[9]

---

[7]Washington Administrative Code 388-561-0100 says that if the trust is created by the disabled client for his/her spouse, not as part of a Will, then it's treated as an available resource and the disabled client must consume the funds before being able to ask for state aid. Check your own state for this complication.

[8]Please read Chapter 8 regarding Medicaid, for a fuller explanation.

[9] See Chapter 3 regarding trusts for children.

Chapter 5: Living Trusts v. Wills

Sometimes clients want a Living Trust. That may be the right choice for you, and it may be the wrong choice. Despite what you may hear on television, or read in the newspaper ads, it is *not* the right choice for everyone. You will have to decide for yourself whether it is the right choice for you. Let's compare the probate process using a Last Will with the Living Trust. I'll warn you in advance that if you are interested in Living Trusts and you have concerns about tax planning, you should read Chapter 9 first, and then come back to this one. If your only concerns are about avoiding probate and protecting privacy, then it will make sense to read this chapter first.

Probate is the orderly process of paying the obligations of the person who died and distributing his or her assets to the people they intended to remember after death. Each person owns their own property until the moment of death; then at death, it transfers to the people named in the *Last Will and Testament*. The Court relies upon the instructions given in the Last Will and Testament telling us who gets what, how taxes are paid, how much flexibility to give the executor, etc. Some states have progressive and easy probate codes, which are designed to give the *Personal Representative* (Executor) the most flexibility possible. Some states have probate codes that are less flexible, and which cause the estate to spend more on settlement fees.

Using the Last Will, the Personal Representative or Executor (generally the surviving spouse) applies to the court for permission to act with non-intervention powers. That means he or she can settle the estate without having to go back to the court for authority for each task. The Personal Representative can usually sell the family home without consulting the court. In some states, the probate file can be closed without even an inventory being published in the court file and without a full accounting. Whatever state you are in, we hope the process will be simple, and done at a reasonable cost.

A Living Trust operates differently. The LivingTrust document is created when the people are still living. Everything they own is transferred to the trust. The trust document directs the trustee (usually the same person, called the "Grantor") to make payments to them from the assets that are invested (stock and bank accounts) and to pay all their bills. Sometimes they choose to have their income put into a trust account and then they write all the checks from the trust account. When they die, the trust directs the next trustee to pay their final bills and to distribute the assets to their heirs. When we ask what the Grantor owned at the moment of death, the answer is "nothing". And if you own nothing then you probably don't have to go through probate court.

You will sometimes hear the trust referred to as the A-B Trust (for people with modest estates) or as the A-B-C Trust (for married people who need more extensive tax planning). In each case, the parties contribute their assets to the trust. Married couples can sign a single trust together, or they can each sign an individual trust. Community property and separate property retain that character. Either party can revoke the trust and take their money and property out of the trust.

The A-B Trust starts out as one trust, A, and continues that way through the time that both partners are living. It holds their community property and their separate property. When the first partner dies, then the trust divides into two trusts. Trust A continues just as it did, but holding only the survivor's portion, providing for the care of the survivor and allowing that partner to dispose of the assets as they desire during life or on his/her death. Remember, the partner who died owned some of the trust assets. That person's portion goes into a new trust, B. It is used to provide for the survivor during life. The surviving spouse can't give the assets in the B trust to anyone and can't revoke that part of the trust. However, the survivor can always revoke his/her own part of the trust, which remains in Trust A. The trust document already tells us who gets the deceased partner's share, which is now in B, after the surviving spouse is gone.

For people needing more tax planning, we use the A-B-C Trust. Again, A is the general trust for the benefit of both or for the survivor. When the first partner dies, we divide the A Trust into two parts: one part owned by the survivor and one part owned by the person who passed on. Then the deceased person's part is divided again, into two portions: the tax free amount (the Credit Shelter Trust) goes into trust B, and the amount over the tax free amount, goes into Trust C. The C Trust is designed to qualify for the marital deduction, because the money can only be spent for the surviving spouse.[10]

In either case, the B Trust will never be taxed, because that is the tax free or exclusionary amount. When the surviving partner dies, he/she will be taxed on the amount which exceeds his/her tax free amount, when combining A and C.

People who have no surviving spouse or partner to worry about can use a trust with just the A portion.

---

[10]You'll read more about the marital trust in Chapter 15. It's a trust that holds assets which are more than the estate tax free amount, and can only provide for the surviving spouse (not the kids). All the income must be given to the surviving spouse, or spent for the spouse's support. If the rules are followed, the funds in the trust are not taxed until the surviving spouse also passes away.

Problems can affect the cost

Keep this in mind: It costs much more to set up a Living Trust than it does to create a Last Will and Testament. That is because all your property has to be transferred to the trust. It takes care of situations that arise during your life and when you die. So, it is twice as much work; expect to pay at least twice as much as you would for a Will. Then throughout your life, the trust will need adjustments, costing more in legal fees.

Some types of situations are going to cost the estate more money than otherwise. Whether there is a Last Will, a Living Trust, or no written directions, there can be problems in any of these situations:

- There is no Will or Living Trust so the Personal Representative doesn't have non-intervention powers and must get court permission to act.

- There is a tax issue and we spend a lot of time dealing with the IRS.

- Somebody has a drinking or a drug problem. It could be the person who died or someone who is left behind; these people cause problems from poor thinking and irrational behavior. This takes more attorney time and the legal bill always reflects that.

- The "girlfriend/boyfriend" problem: the person who died left behind a domestic partner whom they had not married, and now that person wants to have some of the financial benefits of marriage, even though they were not married. Or worse yet, the person who died wanted the partner to have assets, and when the partner makes a claim against the estate to get the assets, the family members oppose it. (See a later chapter on this topic).[11]

- Bickering between the children.

- The beneficiary designations in a retirement or insurance policy don't match those in the Will or Living Trust, so we have to make adjustments to carry out the intent.[12]

- Someone challenges the document claiming the person who died wasn't thinking clearly and didn't understand what they were doing when they signed the Will.

Solving these problems will be time-consuming and cost the estate extra dollars. They don't go away just because there is a Living Trust rather than a Last Will.

Living Trusts for specific purposes

A Living Trust does solve some problems, but only if the problems apply to you! If you live in a state where the probate code is difficult and expensive (California comes to mind), then avoiding probate is a great idea. If you live in a state, where there is a very

---

[11] Please be aware that domestic partners in many states have a claim to the assets that were earned by either of them during the time of their co-habitation. This can be true even if your state does not have a common law marriage statute. If you live with a domestic partner, whether that person is the opposite sex or the same sex, be sure you put into place some sort of property agreement that discusses what each one owns and what happens to that property if you should part. You are acting at your peril if you do not take this advice. This claim applies both during life and to the estate assets at death.

[12]See Chapter 7.

progressive and "user friendly" probate code, you don't need to avoid probate.

Out of state assets

In every state where you own property, you must file a probate case in the court, if you are using a Last Will to transfer property (or if you have no document). If you have property in a different state, then a Living Trust could be the right choice since it is an entity to hold that property only. For example, if you own a beach house in California, but you live and die in Washington, then your Personal Representative will have to open a probate case in California to transfer the beach property and will also have to open another probate in Washington for all the other property. But if you put the property into a Living Trust, then at the moment of death, we ask what you owned in California. The answer is that you owned nothing there. The trust owned the property for your benefit but the trust didn't die! There is no need for a California probate. This is an important benefit to heirs, both financially and emotionally.

Beneficiaries with disabilities

One client came to me in a common predicament:

Her 40-year-old son had been in an accident as a teenager, leaving him with a minor brain injury. It affected both his thinking and his personality. He lived with her, and couldn't hold down even a part time job. Often he would be fired because his bad temper which was a part of his illness. He didn't pay rent or utilities, and he had very little responsibility.

A Will and probate was not a good choice for her. The probate code in most states requires that no money be paid out to the heirs for several months while the creditor claims are coming in. What would her son do during that period? The Executor wouldn't be able to distribute money to him or to let him use the house rent-free.[13]

The better choice was a Living Trust. Her house and all her savings and stocks were put into the trust. She and her daughter were the co-trustees. The daughter was very agreeable to treat the son's bills as the mother's bills. The trustee was directed to pay all the income to the mother during her lifetime. When she died, the new trustee was directed to use the money to pay bills for her son. There was no interruption in the flow of cash to take care of her son. It was a perfect solution to the problem.

Privacy concerns

Another client had an unusual problem:

He was a single man with too many women in his life! He had no wife, but a number of women friends whom he wanted to remember kindly. But he didn't want them to find out about each other, and he didn't want his family to know about any of them!

The Living Trust was a good solution. He had a brokerage account that paid him an income. We put that into the Living Trust, and he remained the trustee. The document directed the trustee to continue paying him the income during his life. When he dies, the new

---

[13] That's not completely true in all situations. If we could prove his disability, then we could use the Family Support Statute (or whatever your state has to take care of disabled children), but that does not work in every case. Some situations lack the evidence to support the claim of disability for an adult child.

trustee will distribute a portion to each of the friends. The trustee is also directed to not deliver a copy of the trust document to any of them and to not reveal the contents to anyone. The rest of his estate will show up in a probate, but no one will know about the trust.

Remember, in some states, no inventory need be published in the court file. The only place the Living Trust will show up is the estate tax return. His heirs are not entitled to a copy of the tax return unless they demand it, and it is not public. But the heirs to the trust are not heirs to the probate estate, so they have no right to demand it. Tax will still be due on the money in the trust. But no one knows, and so his private life remains private.

Taking advantage of the elderly

Another client was rapidly declining:

On Tuesday, she could be fine. Ask her on Friday if she paid the bills, and she may not remember. She had enough sense one Tuesday to recognize that she could be in deep trouble any day. Her husband was deceased. Of her three children, one was living in France, one came over frequently for loans he never repaid, and one, her only daughter, was attentive and loving. A Living Trust was also a perfect solution for this woman. We created a trust in which she and her daughter are the co-trustees. Either one could sign checks and manage her affairs. The mother could stay in control for as long as she was able, and if she didn't do well one week, the daughter could step in. Because the daughter had access to the accounts, she could find out if the borrower-son had been there, and if so, put an end to it.

This is a reason often cited for having a Living Trust. There is a smooth transition from the parent to the caregiver in the declining years. When the time comes for the parent to do less, the caregiver seamlessly moves into position. When the Grantor passes on, there is a smooth flow of assets to the next beneficiary.

The Surviving Spouse May Remarry

The structure of the Living Trust prevents the surviving spouse from distributing the assets to anyone except until the time of death. This safety feature is often a selling point of the Living Trust. A new spouse can't get the money! A salesman can't talk the survivor into spending it. The kids can't beg for it. This is a great planning tool if a spouse is an easy target.

Disaster recovery

A Living Trust has other practical applications for families who are affected by disasters like September 11. Many minor children had at least one parent missing but not declared dead. The estimates in late September were that approximately 350 minor children were left with no parents. Since the parents were not declared dead, there was no way to start a probate to get the court to allow the distribution of funds from the parents' accounts. If there was one surviving spouse, then the survivor could get to accounts, but only if the accounts were in their joint names or if the missing person had left a power of attorney giving someone authority to use their funds. If neither of those situations applied, then the survivors had to depend on the courts to help them out.

Most jurisdictions do not have enough court staff or court-rooms to handle a flood of 5,000 new probate cases or conservatorships, which is what may have happened after the September 11 events. The courts likely would hire temporary judges and run court hours later than usual, and they would do the best they could to find additional courtrooms. But even so, this would take time and coordination. For guardianships, the courts are likely to require a medical examination to prove the individual cannot take care of his or her own affairs. That would be impossible if someone is missing after a terrorist attack.

In such unusual situations, the Last Will and Testament is not as satisfactory a tool as it is in peaceful times, unless there are good Powers of Attorney in place.[14] A co-trustee or a successor trustee in a Living Trust needs to have access to the accounts, even if the missing parent has not been declared dead. A Living Trust can provide that ability, with no waiting period.

Avoiding Tax Liabilities

Some states allow the agent, acting under a Power of Attorney, to change that person's Last Will and Testament if doing it would produce a better tax result for the estate. But other states won't allow that to be part of the power of attorney. However, a Living Trust is not restricted this way. In a time of changing tax codes, its impossible to predict the future. This might be a good reason to select the Living Trust.

Considerations on Re-marriage

People who are re-marrying and who have substantial separate property might consider the Living Trust with just the A portion,

---

[14]See Chapter 6 regarding powers of attorney.

because it puts a fence around their assets. A widowed person who remarries often doesn't want his/her assets from the first marriage to go to the new spouse's children. There cannot be any squabble about who owns what, if the separate property is put into a trust from the beginning. The new spouse cannot add anything to the trust, and cannot take anything from it. It makes a clear definition of ownership.

What the Courts Think

The Living Trust does not have the same standard of review by a court that a Will has. It is not as easy to challenge a Living Trust as it is to challenge a Will. The formalities of a Will require a certain number of witnesses, and usually has a place for a notary public to sign the document saying that all were present and all signed together, and each one saw the others sign. A Living Trust doesn't require that. Since a Living Trust is not a Will, those same requirements won't apply.

Sometimes a client wants to be sure that no one can overcome their wishes expressed in their Will as the final document that gives away their property. They may have a same sex partner and are worried that relatives will try to take property from the partner. Or perhaps they are leaving nothing to the children and want to give it all to charity. A Living Trust is less likely to be successfully challenged.

Summary

Here are some reasons to use a Living Trust, rather than a Will:

•   A Living Trust makes passing your property to the heirs easier if the state where you die has a complex and expensive probate code. It takes care of privacy issues.

- It avoids having to open a separate probate case in order to transfer property outside the state where a person lives.

- It makes assets quickly available for special care problems, such as a disabled child. There is no waiting period for distribution.

- It allows the next trustee to change the trust document to improve the estate tax result.

- It prevents the survivor from giving away all the assets.

Here are things to consider, as you weigh the extra costs of using a Living Trust rather than a Will:

- It won't make the taxes any lower

- It won't keep the children from fighting with each other

- It won't fix a bad decision before or after death

- It won't make the girlfriend go away without money.

A Living Trust may be the right thing for your situation. Only you can judge whether the extra cost of setting up the trust is worth its purchase.

Finally, be aware that there are unscrupulous individuals and companies that want to sell you a Living Trust for a very high price. They may say that lawyers charge too much, that you will pay less tax if you have the trust, and that probate costs are much too high. Don't fall for their scare tactics. Choose the Living Trust only if its right for you.

Chapter 6: **Powers of Attorney/Health Care Directives**

If you get sick or are in an accident, somebody has to make decisions about your health, about who will visit you, about which doctor will take care of you, about how to handle your money. Just like a Will, the State Legislature has already made some decisions for you. Again, you may like what they selected or, you may not. I personally don't like the choices that the legislature made for me. I have somebody else in mind. We call the person you select the *Agent,* or the *Attorney in Fact.*

For a long while, my kids were too young to handle these decisions by themselves. I named my sister, but she had to consult with my two oldest children. After my kids were in their twenties, I named my sister and my two oldest children, but they had to consult the youngest child. One day I talked with my sister. She'd had some surgery. She went into the surgery not knowing what was wrong. So she told the doctor to take out anything he wanted; it was all okay with her. Stunned, I asked her if she'd gotten another opinion. She laughed and said she trusted him! Well, I wasn't laughing. I wanted another opinion if it was me. I always joke about how I fired her the next day. It's not that she made the wrong decision. The problem is that she made a decision in a way that was so different from the way I would make it. I'd have gotten another opinion.

Even with someone you trust to make your health care decisions, there are some things that need to be spelled out to your Agent. If you're going to die, should we give you everything to prolong your life, or let you pass on naturally? If there is a pregnancy, should your body be kept alive long enough to deliver the baby? Do you want unconventional pain treatment? Your Agent is obligated to try to figure out what you want, so you should probably have this in writing.

Somebody needs to manage your money if you are sick.

Remember, one day you may be well again, and you still want money to be there. This means your eighteen-year-old son isn't suitable (you can't believe how many people suggest their young son or daughter). Do you have a business? Maybe the person handling your home finances should be different from the person who is handling your business finances. You have to tell the world in writing, or no one can prove what you want or don't want.

One of my clients was widowed, and although he had brothers and sisters and a young adult son, he chose his wife's sister as the Agent. Several years after we prepared his Power of Attorney, he was in a motorcycle accident. He went straight from the hospital to the nursing home, where he stayed for a month. When he finally got home, he couldn't handle the bills at all. His wonderful sister-in-law came to the rescue and did everything. She was busy collecting his disability pay, arranging time off from his work, paying the bills. She took great care of him and he was grateful. She wasn't his closest relative or the one he was most friendly with. However, she was the best choice he could have made.

An attorney friend of mine had a client in a guardianship case. The man was single, and had a motorcycle accident, but he didn't have any documents telling us who could manage his affairs. His young son, aged about 25, went to the Court and asked to be appointed as the guardian. So did the Dad's former girlfriend. Yes, you read that correctly. The former girlfriend wanted to be his guardian. Apparently she thought she knew enough about the business from "pillow talk" to know how to run it. She made a good case and the Court considered her as a possible guardian. The moral of this story is that you need some plans. Someone has to take care of you, your money, your health. You are doing yourself and your family a favor if you select those people in advance.

You are also saving yourself a lot of money. A guardianship case is not for the "faint of wallet". If no one has been appointed to handle your legal and financial affairs for you, then the Court must appoint someone. No doubt, somebody will show up and say the appropriate words, asking to be appointed as the guardian. How will the Court know if that person is honest, has money problems of his own, has been bullying you, or whether that person has neglected you for years? The Court will try to find out, because the Court will appoint someone to act as "the eyes and ears" of the Court. That person is called the Guardian ad Litem. Usually the Guardian ad Litem is an attorney. Its his/her job to interview everybody in the family and network of friends, to review medical reports, to look over the finances. Then the Guardian ad Litem will report back to the Court and make a recommendation. So who is paying for all this work? You are! A Petition for Guardianship, with the Guardian ad Litem, followed by several hearings, and without even a trial (which you get if you contest the appointment of the guardian) could easily cost $5,000 (an estimated amount for Seattle in 2006). If there are several contenders to be your guardian, then its much more. You could probably get your Wills and powers of attorney prepared for less than half of that, including tax planning and trusts for the kids.

The most cost efficient way of handling your affairs, and the path that is most likely to get you the guardian you really trust, is to prepare documents, in advance of the disaster, that say what you want. You should have these documents:

- a Health Care Directive (also called a Living Will) which tells what kind of care you want if you are terminally ill. You might also use a document called "The Five Wishes", which is more descriptive about all kinds of choices during the time you are ill or passing away.

- a Health Care Power of Attorney, allowing someone to have the power to act for you in making health care arrangements (i.e., Shall we change physicians? Should we use alternative treatments?) and getting medical records.

- a General Durable Power of Attorney, allowing someone to have the power to make your legal and financial decisions.

Chapter 7: Passing Assets Outside Your Probate Estate

The point of the stories in this chapter is to let you know that your estate plan is not complete without updating your retirement accounts. What you said in your Last Will needs to match your intentions regarding the beneficiary designations on your bank accounts, on your life insurance, and on your retirement accounts. Some assets like these are passed along outside the estate, and they are not covered by your Will, so they don't follow the orders you've put in your Will. That's because the beneficiary designations are "mini-Wills". Don't leave this out of the discussion with your lawyer.

Individual Retirement Accounts and 401(k) Accounts

Retirement accounts can be accumulated in many forms. They can be "defined benefits" which means that the employer pays a set amount of money after your retirement, for your life or for the life of you and your spouse (whichever you choose). I will not discuss the defined benefits because they end at death and are not inherited.

This discussion is about the other retirement that comes in the form of a benefit from work, which pays you an amount based on the accumulations and earnings. If you work for a company, their benefits may be paid into a 401(k) fund. If you work for a non-profit entity, then it's paid into a 403(b) fund. These are the names of the tax codes regulating the tax benefits of retirement accounts. Individual Retirement Accounts (IRA's) come about in several ways. Either the company you work for accumulates the money into an account during your working years, or, you may choose to accumulate additional money yourself, in an account away from work. Some companies accumulate the money for you in a retirement fund, then at your retirement, the company transfers the money to an IRA for you. You must then manage it yourself.

When I speak in this chapter about IRAs or 401(k)s, although they are very different products, the discussion applies to all of them.

Conflict between IRA/401(k)designation and Will

Rick was self-motivated and very successful. He didn't think he needed a lawyer to help with his Will. He was a self-made man, and knew what to do. He bought a standard-form will at the stationery store and filled in the details. His Will said that everything should be split equally between the two sons. Despite his best efforts at protecting his estate, he had made a common mistake that might have created a disaster.

Rick had two sons. When he started his IRA savings, one son was 18 and the other was 12. He named the elder son the beneficiary of the IRA, and put a statement in his will that the IRA should be split equally between the two sons. He contributed to the IRA until the younger son turned 21. During that time, he invested only in Microsoft stock. He was a very lucky man: the stock split three times, and the little investment he had put there turned into $800,000. When the younger son turned 21, Rick opened a new IRA account, naming the younger son as the beneficiary. When Rick died, it only had $17,000. So here's the question: when Rick died, which directions controlled the distribution: IRA designations or the Will?

The IRA/401(k)designation or any designation for bank accounts, retirement, or life insurance prevails over a Will or a Living Trust. And this can be a problem. Many times, an individual forgets about a designation he/she made several years ago. Or, like many the young families, they name a relative to receive the money, trusting they'll do the right thing.

One problem is that the brokerage company which is managing

the IRA or 401(k), isn't free to hand out retirement money without reporting it to the IRS. That money has never been taxed as income[15], so someone has to pay the tax when the money is withdrawn. When a beneficiary is named, there is a limited time for the person to withdraw the funds. The IRS wants to know who that beneficiary is and when they are withdrawing the money. Withdrawal of the funds always attracts a tax.

Complications from IRA/401(k)tax liability

Mike had a long-term companion and he wanted to provide for her if he died first. He had few assets other than his individual retirement account (his IRA). He named his two grown children as the beneficiaries of the IRA account. To purchase a condo, he withdrew $250,000 from the IRA. He didn't pay any income tax at the time he withdrew those funds. He probably figured he'd withdraw more money to pay the income tax when it was due in April of the following year. He put the condominium in joint ownership with his lady companion.

Next, he went to his lawyer, and he told her to write a Will naming his children as the beneficiaries of his estate, subject to the companion being able to use the condominium for the remainder of her life. He didn't tell the lawyer about the outstanding tax due on the IRA withdrawal.

Mike died in December. The companion owned half the condominium, and the children owned his half, subject to the companion being able to use it for her lifetime. His probate estate did not include his IRA accounts. Those went directly to the children. The children would have been required to let the companion live in the condominium, and they would have sold

---

[15] If it's a Roth IRA or Roth 401(k), then the tax has already been paid.

it when she died. Unfortunately, the income tax was still owed on the original $250,000 withdrawal he used to buy the condominium. There were not enough probate assets to pay the income tax. The IRA passed outside the Will so it couldn't be used to pay the income tax. The only way to get the tax paid was to sell the condominium and use the proceeds for the tax payment. The companion to used her half of the proceeds to buy a smaller and less comfortable place to live. Mike's plan for the companion to have the use of that particular condominium for her lifetime failed.

IRA/401(k) is not a substitute for a Will

And here's the worst story of all. Monica and Steve, both in their early 30's, had two small children. They had no Will when they suddenly died in an auto accident. Together they had retirement accounts and insurance totaling $200,000. It all went to Steve's mother through their beneficiary designations, with her verbal promise that she'd use the money to take care of the children. When Monica and Steve died, she withdrew the IRA account all at once (very bad tax move) and she put it in a stock account in her own name.

Tragedy struck again. Steve's mother died unexpectedly a few years later, and her will said that everything should go to her own living children, Steve's siblings. She had never put anything into writing about Steve's children or where the stock account came from. Now if the siblings had been kinder, they would have settled upon some plan of transferring that money into trust for Steve and Monica's children. The brothers and sisters dug in their greedy heels and refused to acknowledge that the money was intended for Monica and Steve's children. They received their father's share of his mother's estate, but they didn't get back the money that their parents had left in her care.

Actually, there *is* a worse story. It's the common story about the parents who left the money to their spouses first, and if they didn't survive, to the children. As soon as the little guys turn 18, ready or not, they get the money handed to them. Let me remind you that 18 year olds are in the middle of their senior year of high school (translation: not ready). It happens all the time. I've tried to convince the judge that the guardians should be able to delay the transfer by purchasing an annuity that pays out in stages, paying for college, and delaying the rest until the child is older. I've tried, but I've not had a successful result. The law says that 18 is a legal adult, and the child is entitled to his money, ready or not. This is a terrible substitute for a Will or Living Trust.

You thought your IRA/401(k)was yours?

If you have an IRA or a 401(k) package, or any other retirement arrangement, your name is on the account. You are the wage earner. You probably think that makes it yours. You are incorrect, if you are married. You probably think it's yours, even if you earned it before the marriage. Again, you are incorrect. I have a very unhappy client who discovered after marrying his second wife that the half million dollar account he earned before the marriage, goes to his new wife, unless she agrees to let someone else inherit it...... and she's not going to!

This is a complicated area, and there are tax attorneys who specialize in retirement benefits law. So if you think this affects you, hire someone to help you through this maze! If the account was provided by your employer, then you have to follow the rule I gave you, above (it goes to your spouse on death unless your spouse signs the designation, saying it can go to someone else). If the account was not funded by your employer, then you might be able to give it to someone else without your spouse's permission. This depends upon a host of factors that I will not outline here. But if you want to give the account to someone other than a spouse, and the IRS rules allow that without the spouse's signature, you still have another hurdle to climb.

Most of the brokerage companies holding the accounts don't want to be involved with the details of your life, nor do they want litigation with your surviving spouse about what you can or can't do with the account. As a result, the companies have written statements, called the Custodial Agreement, which you sign when you open the accounts. You have to check two documents from your account manager (usually a stock brokerage company) to see if you can make the gift of the retirement account to someone other than your spouse. First go to the Custodial Agreement. In that document, there are rules about who gets your money when you pass on. If you are married, in almost every case, the Custodial Agreement says that you must leave it to your spouse if you pass on, unless the spouse waives the rule. If you use that company, you must follow its rule. This will probably be true, *even if* the account was not funded by your employer (in which case, the IRS would allow you to leave it to someone other than your spouse).

You must next look at the beneficiary designation form. This can be misleading. It may say that your spouse must sign if you are leaving it to someone other than the spouse. But it may not say anything about a spouse's consent. So you may have a false belief that you can leave it to anyone. This is a trap for the unwary! Check both documents carefully!

A brokerage company has only one job: to make money for you. They don't want to defend you in a lawsuit, so they make it simple for themselves. Follow their rules or invest somewhere else. I give you two warnings here. First, if this is an issue, you should address it up front with your intended spouse, before the marriage, and put it in a prenuptial agreement. Second, check both the beneficiary designation form and the Custodial Agreement before you enter marriage. Once married, your spouse will probably have to consent if you want to leave it to someone else, even if the IRS rules would allow it. There is much more detail to this subject. Get expert help!

New rules on IRAs

The rules on retirement account distributions changed in 2001. You now have less trouble leaving your accounts to your heirs. And it is important to know that you can leave your IRA/401(k)accounts to a trust for the benefit of your children. You don't need to leave it to Mom or your best friend hoping they'll do the right thing. You can put on the beneficiary designation form that the account is given to the trustee, in the trust created for the benefit of your children, or whomever you want.

Designations for retirement benefits and life insurance should match the Will or the Living Trust. People often tell me that they believe the designations are null and void once they sign a Will. Work with your broker or account manger to complete the designation forms. Each company has its own rules about how to do this. Don't guess! Either work with the those people, or hire an attorney or accountant to help you do this. As you will see below, there may be a tax consequence to the designations.

If Rick had understood what could go wrong between his sons, he would have moved money between the two IRA accounts, equalizing them between the sons, and then making all future contributions in equal shares to the two accounts. Mike might have divided his IRA account into three parts: one part for each of his children, and one to take care of his final expenses including the tax. Then the tax due on the money he withdrew to purchase the condominium money would have been available and his sweetheart might have been able to live there for her lifetime. And Steve and Monica, like all young parents reading this, should have done a Will or Living Trust first, and then made sure the beneficiary designations named a trustee to handle the money for their children, instead of designating Mom personally as the owner.

Time Limits on making withdrawals

There is another reason you have to carefully state your beneficiary designations for your retirement assets. The IRS allows us to put away money for our old age. So, we are allowed to put off paying tax on the money until we withdraw it. Remember our discussion about the tax system rewarding socially acceptable behaviors.

But the IRS does not want the heirs to create a tax-free account that stays open beyond your heirs natural life expectancy. That's too much of a benefit. So, when a taxpayer dies, there is a time limit on how long the heirs can delay taking the money out of the retirement account.

If your spouse is the beneficiary, then the spouse can do a *roll-over*. That means he or she can simply transfer the assets into his or her own IRA account. The spouse can leave the money in the account, with no forced withdrawals, until his or her own retirement. It's treated as though the spouse had earned it. The obvious advantage is that the assets continue to accumulate income without being taxed until the surviving spouse retires. When the inheriting spouse dies, the IRA can be transferred to the children.

If you name anyone besides the spouse as the beneficiary, then the rules change. The heirs are forced to withdraw the money, and when the money is withdrawn, the income tax on that money is due. Remember, it has never been taxed. If you select people as your beneficiaries (instead of organizations), there are two choices for withdrawing the money:

1. The automatic option is to withdraw it within five years. The beneficiary can withdraw in any amounts he/she desires. It doesn't matter as long as the money is out of the account in the next five years. Every withdrawal is added to the beneficiary's other income for that

year. If the account has $100,000, and your heir takes it out in equal five payments, she adds $20,000 to her income in each year. Adding that money to her income might push her into a higher tax bracket. If she takes it all out in the first year, she'll probably pay an even higher tax rate.

2. Individuals can choose an alternate way to withdraw the money: they can take the money out over a period equal to their remaining lifetimes. The IRS uses a life expectancy table, but to make this easy, let's assume for these examples that the life expectancy for everybody is 96 years. If your sister is 36 when you die and she inherits your IRA, then we presume she'll live another 60 years. She can choose to take out the money over her lifetime (making an "election"), and withdraw $1/60^{th}$ of the total fund the first year. Then the next year, she'll withdraw 1/59th of the total fund. This may be a good choice. Adding the smaller amount of money to her income might not move her into a higher tax bracket. This is referred as the "stretch-out" of the retirement assets. [16]

If you leave the money to a non-human being, the rules change. Non-human beings include your estate, charities, trusts, and so on. The five-year rule applies; there is no option to withdraw the money over a longer period. This is a problem if the beneficiary doesn't want to take the money immediately and wants the money to continue earning income tax-free over the longest possible period.

---

[16]This opportunity is only available if the sponsoring employer plan allows for withdrawal of the funds over a long period of time. In some companies, the money must be withdrawn within a very short time. Congress passed a new rule in 2006 that allows the heir of a 401K plan, with this company limitation, to roll the amount over into an IRA with the stretch-out opportunity.

Naming the Children's Trustee as the Beneficiary

There is a specific exception to the five year rule, if you designate a trust as the beneficiary. A trust would ordinarily be a non-human entity. If the trust specifically names the people who are the beneficiaries ("my children"), then the IRS will allow the trust to be treated as a person.

If you set up the trust for the benefit of your three children, the IRS will treat the trust as if it were specifically designated to the human beneficiaries, and allow the trustee to select a withdrawal time using the life expectancy of the oldest in the group. If the deceased had minor children and was a working person, the guardian will get Social Security for the children's care until they are 18. So, the trustee may not need the IRA money now. This means that the trustee may take the minimum IRA withdrawals and add them to the trust funds to increase the trust's earned income. However, the majority of the money stays in the IRA, earning income and not paying any tax.

If, instead, you name your estate, rather than the children's trust, as the beneficiary, then the estate must withdraw the money within five years. That creates a huge difference in the amount of money that is allowed to accumulate tax free. Be sure you discuss this with your estate planner. Don't rely upon the people in your benefits office to give you the answer with the best tax advantage.

Remember these basics

This is the basic information that I'd like to leave with you:

1. You should usually leave your retirement funds to your spouse directly (assuming that's who you want to get it) rather than your estate. If you leave the money to your "estate" , even if you gave directions

that all of your estate goes to your spouse, the five-year rule will apply. You don't want the limitation of the five-year rule to apply if you can get the spousal rollover, with a longer distribution time.

2. Always try to name specific people as the beneficiaries, unless you are naming a trust which names specific people as the beneficiaries. This allows them to make the election to *stretch out* the withdrawals over their lifetimes. Since the IRS will require a lifetime withdrawal using the life expectancy of the eldest in the group, it's better to have a trust for each one, or a separate account for each one, so each can use his/her own life expectancies as the calculator.

3. Think carefully about when your youngsters should get money outright, and if they are too young, name a trustee of the trust you create for them, as the beneficiary.

4. The distribution rules are different depending on whether or not the wage earner had already begun taking withdrawals from the retirement account. So the designations are done differently, depending on this distinction.

You can see that distributing retirement assets is not an easy task, and it is worth your time to check with your financial planner or your attorney to make sure everything works together.[17] This never

---

[17] Don't rely solely on the people in your company's human resources or benefits office as the final source of advice on this. They are not estate planners. They may prefer that you name your designated heir

53

mattered when employees had defined benefit packages and the employees received retirement pension for life. Those days are mostly over. When you leave the company, it converts your retirement package into an IRA and you are sent on your way with a good luck wish. It's up to you to make sure it is done right. Save your heirs grief - do it right.

---

using a computer form, or by using a prepared form that gives you only their own list of choices. Ask your lawyer or your financial planner to help maneuver this difficult trek.

Chapter 8: **Long Term Care and Medicaid Planning**

Many of my clients are middle class family people. They work hard, pay their bills, raise their children and hope to someday have enough to retire. The big stickler for the married couples is the fact that they may face long term care in a nursing home. They know that they've got enough money to care for themselves for awhile. They also know that if they spend all the money on the first spouse who gets sick, then the second partner won't have enough to live out his/her life comfortably.

The statistics are daunting. Of all the people over 65, 70% will need long term care or home care, in some form, before they pass away. The average length of care is 2.4 years. In 2004, the average cost of long term care was $58,000 per year in a facility or $23,000 per year for care at home.[18]

Naturally, you can pay for your care, using your funds. I'm going to suggest three other solutions to the problem: relying on your family for care, getting the government to take care of you, or buying long term care insurance.

Counting on Your Family

First, you can live with your children. I like this solution. I used to take care of them, and I think they should have to take care of me later. The only trouble is that I might need full time nursing care, and they go to work every day. Maybe their spouses like me, but then maybe they don't like me enough to take me into their homes, when I am sick and frail. Although this is the best plan, it's risky for me to count on it. They have their own lives to live.

---

[18] "The National Nursing Home Survey," National Center for Health Statistics, U.S. Department of Health and Human Services, June 2003.

The choice of having children care for their elders is the best one, by far. When my mother was ill, we were lucky to have family who had room for her, welcomed her, who didn't need to go to work every day, and were generous enough to give up time to care for a sick person. Every family does not have this luxury.

Getting the State to Take Care of You

The second solution is to organize life around the Medicaid rules[19]. It's not cheap to live in assisted living or in a nursing home. Think in terms of around $6,000 per month in 2006. The state will pay for your care in an assisted living facility or in a nursing home if you don't have enough of your own money. You have to be eligible, considering both your income and your available resources. **Before we begin, you need to understand this clearly: These are the current rules, in Washington state. The rules will be similar in other states, but perhaps not identical. You MUST check with an attorney in your own state, to review the rules if you decide to use this option. The rules change all the time, and each state has its own way of implementing federal requirement.**

Your income must be fully used to support your care, with a few exceptions. You can keep about $50 for personal care items. You can continue to pay for spousal support (described below), health care insurance and for medical bills incurred prior to eligibility for Medicaid.[20] Other than that, you must contribute all of your funds to

---

[19]In Washington, if you get help from the state for long term care, its called Medicaid. In California, its called MediCal. Wherever you live, just substitute your state's name for this process.

[20]This is only a list of the major rules. You must get assistance figuring out all the details as they relate to your particular situation.

your care. So what will your spouse live on? Your spouse can keep all the income which is paid in his/her name. The Medicaid spouse can give spousal support to the healthy spouse, so that the healthy spouse has a minimum income, between $1604 to $2,500[21] per month (depending on the cost of shelter). The spouse can live in the family home until his/her death, then the state will file its lien, demanding to be repaid for the money it advanced. Remember, when the state gives money for your care and you own a home, the state isn't making a gift to you. It's making a loan.[22]

In addition to income, the state will consider whether you have *available resources* that can be converted to cash, so that you can pay your own bills. If you have a home and you believe you may return to it when you are well, then it will not be counted as an available resource for your care, unless the equity is over $500,000[23] and you are single. When you are gone, however, the state will put a lien on the home and your heirs can't sell it without repaying the state. If you are married, you may transfer the home to your spouse and it will not be treated as an available resource. [24] You may also transfer other assets to your spouse, up to $99,540[25]. The state will not honor prenuptial agreements keeping assets separate, so if you marry and have separate assets that you acquired before the marriage, remember that you will

---

[21]This is the amount in Washington state, 2006.

[22]Keep reading! This only applies if you are single.

[23]Each state currently has the right to raise this amount to $750,000.

[24]There are additional rules that allow transfers to a sibling or a child who provided care in the home, trusts for the benefit of the spouse, etc. This list is not a complete one.

[25]This is the amount you may transfer prior to applying for Medicaid. If you apply for Medicaid first, you can only transfer $43,943 (2006).

still have to spend down your own assets to about $43,000 if your new spouse needs Medicaid support. The Medicaid applicant may only keep about $2,000 in his/her own name to be eligible. You can have a modest car, a simple burial plan and a small insurance policy. You can also buy an annuity for yourself or your spouse. [26] You will have to cash out your IRA or 401(k) plan.

What should you do if you have more than the allowable available resources and you want to use the resources for something other than your care? First, pay down the mortgage. If you need cash later, you can get a home equity loan, because a loan is not considered an available resource, if you spend it right away. Next, you can buy some of the things I've described above, such as an annuity for yourself or your spouse.

For example, if you've got a house and some stocks or a retirement account that are together worth $600,000, then you have "available resources" to pay for your care for 100 months (almost nine years, assuming you sell the house to pay for your care) in assisted living home, or in a nursing home using your own money. You'll also need doctors, medications, physical therapy. You'll want some clothing, and television. So in this example, you'd have less than the amount needed for nine years of care. When you've used all of your available resources, then the state will pay the difference between the costs of care and your income.

At this point, its pretty simple: use your assets (referred to as "spend down"), then ask the state to pay for the rest of your expenses for life. The down side is that you won't have money for anything that the state doesn't cover. Say goodbye to the cell phone, Christmas presents for the grandkids, massages, poker money, or medical care

---

[26]There are exceptions to this rule, so check the details before purchasing an annuity

that is beyond the basics. You are really at the mercy of the state regarding what care you will receive, because there are limits on what the state will provide.

If you've got a spouse, then the plan of "spend down" is not attractive. Spend all your money, and your spouse is now left with limited resources (limited income described above, the home and about $43,000 in other assets). However, this may be a good plan for the right couple. Look at this example of a good spend down plan:

Rebecca and Stan had no children and were in their early 50s. Rebecca had Multiple Sclerosis for many years and they came to see me when Rebecca started to lose memory. She could barely speak or see, could walk just enough to get herself into the bathroom, and couldn't take her own medications. However, she was competent to understand the financial issues. Stan desperately needed to have someone help with her care, but his salary in a factory didn't allow for that expense. Rebecca was alone from the time he left in the morning until around noon, when a relative came to stay for a few hours. She was alone again for a few hours until Stan got home from work.

His sister finally insisted that they get some help. The problem was that, according to the state's rules, they had "too much" income and "too many available resources". Neither was really true, but they were accurate using the state's guidelines. Stan had been squirreling away a few dollars each payday because he knew one day he'd have to pay for outside help. For the same reason, he didn't spend a dime to keep the house repairs up and didn't sign up at work for retirement and extra health coverage. We had to get his income and assets lower, in order to qualify for the state's benefits. To get less income, Stan enrolled in his retirement plan and insurance plan at work, both of which were deducted from his income. It lowered his take home pay, but the only thing he really had to give up was his savings program. To get rid of the assets, we convinced him to take the savings and pay down the mortgage. Although this was frightening to him, he was assured by the bank that he could get a home equity loan if he needed that money for Rebecca's emergencies (a loan is not an available resource if it's spent right away). He cashed out Rebecca's life insurance, and made all the home improvements that he'd been avoiding for years. We transferred the house into Stan's name alone. Rebecca's IRA was worth $10,000. That was cashed out, and the money was also used to pay down the mortgage. Now that Stan's income was reduced and they had no savings, and Rebecca had no life insurance or retirement assets, they qualified for a state paid chore worker to come into the home while Stan was at work. We did one more thing: we wrote a Will in which Stan left nothing to his wife (remember, he owned the house at that point). He left everything, including the home, to his wife's sister, as the trustee of a Special Needs Trust.[27] If Stan died before Rebecca, then the home would be sold and the funds will be used to pay for the extra things that Rebecca needed.

If "spend down" isn't right for your situation, and there is still money left, then you can give the assets away to someone besides your spouse, but that solution has a few snares. There are new gifting restrictions passed by Congress in February 2006.[28] In order to receive

---

[27]See Chapter 4. Be aware that putting the funds into a Living Trust in Washington will make the funds an available resource, even if Stan dies! You must fund this kind of a trust for a disabled spouse, by using a Will, not a Living Trust. WAC 388-561-0100

[28]The federal rules described here took effect February 6, 2006. Some states have delayed the application of the rules for a short time.

federal money, the state must follow the federal rules about eligibility. The state will look at the date the person becomes eligible for Medicaid (ie, he/she needs care and has less than $2,000, modest car, etc.). If he/she made a gift of assets in the prior five year period, there is a period of ineligibility, and the Medicaid application will be denied. The ineligibility begins on the date when the person would otherwise be eligible, except for the gift (i.e., he/she has less than $2,000, insufficient income, etc.). Divide the total amount of the gifts by $6,000, the current average monthly cost of nursing home care.[29] That is the number of months of future ineligibility. This is tricky: we look at the gifts in the five years before applying for Medicaid. Then the ineligibility period is for future months. The examples below will help you understand the rule.

There may be a penalty for those who received the gifts and refuse to spend it for the Medicaid patient's care.[30] The state will pay the bill, rather than have the individual be denied care. However, if the people who received the gift refuse to pay for care, they will be given a 150% civil penalty for the amount which the state has to pay during that period of ineligibility. Check your own state's rules before making or accepting a gift.

Here is an example:

Mary is a single woman with children. She has $122,000 in cash, and she gives away $120,000 on January 1, 2007, to her children. On February 1, 2009, she applies for Medicaid. She has only $2,000 in her own name, no other assets and for purposes of this example, we will assume she has no income. If not for the gift she made, she would become eligible for

---

[29]Again, these figures are for Washington state, and are current in 2006. You must check the amounts periodically for your state.

[30] RCW74.39A.160 and WAC 388-513-1363(7)

services on February 1, 2009. Her gift of $120,000 divided by the average cost of nursing home care, $6,000, equals 20, and so Mary is ineligible for 20 months. Her ineligibility begins February 1, 2009, the day she applied for Medicaid (that's the day she had insufficient income and not enough available resources, except for the gift she made previously). She will be eligible to receive Medicaid benefits on November 1, 2010, 20 months later. Her children need to pay her expenses for the 20 month period. If they don't, the state will still take care of the bill, but the children will be held liable for the 150% penalty. The result is that the gift didn't preserve her assets.

The following is an example of someone who is able to follow the rules for gifting and still take advantage of the state's resources.

Dan is a single man who has no children. He has an income of $5,000 per month. His nursing home care will cost $7,000. He has a shortfall of $2,000 per month. On January 1, 2007, he keeps only the allowable $2,000, and gives the rest of his assets to his nephew. The gift is $210,000. The state will calculate the period of ineligibility by dividing the gift, $210,000, by the average monthly rate of the cost of nursing home care, $6,000.[31] That results in a period of ineligibility for 35 months.

Dan enters a nursing home on February 1, 2009. During the next 35 months, starting on February 1, 2009, the nephew uses the money he received as a gift to pay the $2,000 shortfall between the cost of nursing home care and his uncle's income. At the end of that time, the nephew has paid out $70,000, and he is able to keep the remaining $140,000. In the

---

[31]Remember, these are the current figures for Washington state. They will change over time, and the figures will be different in other states.

36th month, January 1, 2012, an application for Medicaid is prepared for Dan. It will be approved.

The difference in the results for people like Mary and Dan is the amount of income that the applicant has.

Please remember these points about using state Medicaid!

- First, these rules are complicated. I've only given an outline, and every state has its own rules. Get help before embarking on a gifting plan or a spend down plan.

- Second, a prenuptial agreement will not protect the healthy spouse from the bills of the Medicaid spouse. You may need to either decide to spend down as I've described, or get a "Medicaid Divorce" if you want to preserve your funds.

- Third, all of your assets will be required to be cashed out unless there is a listed exception. You must cash out life insurance, retirement accounts, etc. Very little, except the home, is protected.

- Fourth, if you have a spouse who needs or will need Medicaid, transfer the home to the healthy spouse and have the healthy spouse write a new Will, with a trust to provide for the extra needs of the Medicaid spouse. Leave nothing to the Medicaid spouse outright.

I am going to be very honest about the solution of getting the state to take care of you. It is going to bankrupt America. We have not yet designed an efficient method of caring for those who have nursing home care needs, or disabilities. We have an aging population. Our current method of handing this issue is woefully inadequate. My job is to give you advice; it's not my job to manage the resources of the United States government. I have talked about this particular solution because it's legal (presuming you follow the rules carefully), available, and because clients need it. But as a nation, we should all be concerned about this option.

Long Term Care Insurance

Maybe the examples above present a solution that seems right for you. But if not, you had better make other plans for your old age and long term care. So let's go on to the third option. You can purchase long term care insurance, which will pay for your care while you are in a nursing home or an assisted living facility, or provide care for you in your own home. Each company has its own plan, with various kinds of benefits. Once insured, the insurance company must pay the benefits if the insured person cannot perform two of the six Activities of Daily Living, also called ADL's (bathing, continence, dressing, eating, toileting and transferring from bed to chair), or, if the insured person is severely cognitively impaired, then the insurance must pay, regardless of the ADL's[32].

Here are some of the things to look at when you evaluate a policy:

• The amount of time in a nursing home that will be covered.

The average time needed in a nursing home is 2.4 years, but the agents I spoke with recommend that you purchase 5 years of coverage if you can. The reasons?

---

[32] This is true if the policy is a tax qualified policy, and most of them are.

First, 5 years of coverage will generally cover 91% of the time needed for long term care. Second, if you have Alzheimer's Disease, you could be in a care facility for a long time, with everything but your memory in good shape.

- Inflation

  Find out if there is an inflation or cost of living provision. If so, is it compounded inflation protection or simple inflation protection?

- Exactly what will the policy cover? Ask about these:

  Adult Day Care
  Hospice
  Structural Improvements at your home (for instance, will the policy pay for remodeling in your home if you stay there, and if the home currently does not accommodate a wheelchair?)
  Elimination period for payment of services (30-60-90 days)
  Pre-existing conditions
  Increases in premiums due to inflation
  Maximum daily rate v. the monthly pooled amount
  Discount if your spouse is also covered by the same company
  Medical Alert Systems
  Pre-approval of service, or the "plan of care" established by your physician
  Alternate Services (for instance, can you start with home health care then switch to nursing home care)

- Premium Waiver

    If you need care and no longer have your monthly income, will they waive the premiums?

    Look at the numbers as you analyze this problem. Assume you need $58,000 today for care per year. Two years of care would cost $116,000. How much would you need to have available for your care, if you were in a nursing home for 2 years in the future? Assuming 5% after-tax growth, 5% inflation, here's what you'd need in lump sum or in monthly savings to meet your needs:

Needed in Future	Lump Sum Needed	Monthly Sum You Must Save
5 years	$151,750	$2,046
10 years	$193,676	$1,165
15 years	247,185	$ 876

    All of this presumes that you can calculate how soon you will need the long term care, and it assumes that inflation and growth factors are the same as what I have calculated. Now you need to ask yourself what it would cost to purchase a long term care policy. You'll have to weigh the monthly payment, your wish to preserve your other assets, your risk factors (Alzheimers in the family, longevity in the family), etc. In the end, you really need to talk all of this over with an insurance agent who handles long term care. This is a very specialized insurance. If your employer offers this as an optional benefit, look into it. If not, you owe it to yourself and your family to call an agent and get some quotes. Otherwise, you must rely upon one of the first two options at the beginning of this chapter.

Part Two - Tax Planning

Chapter 9: **The Credit Shelter Trust**

When first written, the tax on the transfer of wealth was intended to affect the very rich. But the estate tax, as we found it at the beginning of 2001, was affecting many who were not rich. In 2001, the tax applied to a person who died owning assets of more than $675,000. In 2001, this was not rich! The average engineer who retires from Boeing generally has acquired that, when you add up home equity, life insurance, savings, and a retirement package (401(k) and IRAs). No wonder Middle Class America was screaming for a revised estate tax.

In June, 2001, Congress responded to the public outcry about the tax with new estate tax legislation. The gift and estate tax code, as we know it today, will apply until 2009; after that, there will be no estate tax. Then a new type of death tax may apply. Congress wrote the new tax bill so that either the new bill takes effect or we revert to the current law. Congress must ratify the new law or it will revert to the prior law. I listen to commentators who are close to the Congress, and rumors fly, with ideas of how the final estate tax bill will look. Last year, I would have predicted that there would be a continuing estate tax, as we know it now, with the tax starting at $10 million. My prediction from late 2006, considering the costs of the war on terrorism and the reconstruction costs after Hurricane Katrina in 2005, is that the tax will hit those with $5 million. But I have no looking glass! You will have to stay alert for future news.

General tax policy is driven by two goals: One is to raise money for the treasury, and the other is to motivate people to act in ways that benefit the public. For instance, home ownership produces stable neighborhoods, a tax base for schools, local interest in improvements, etc. So, the government allows a tax deduction for the interest you pay on your home loan. Charities organize public services like hospital care for the poor, education for disabled persons, and foster care for homeless children. When you give money to those organizations, it relieves the financial pressure on the charities and the government doesn't have to take on the responsibilities. You get a tax deduction as encouragement to make the donation.

The IRS Code applies tax to gifts made during your life or at your death. Any gifts you make above a specified amount will be taxed on a rising scale, from 35% - 49%.

How much money can you have before the government applies a gift or death tax? Right now, it is a shifting number.[33] This chart shows the tax year, the tax-free amount, and the resulting credit against the tax that is due on that amount:

Tax Year	Tax-free Amount	Resulting Credit
2002-2003	$1 million	$345,800
2004-2005	$1.5 million	$555,800
2006, 2007, 2008	$2 million	$780,800
2009	$3.5 million	$1,525,800

This example explains the chart: if a person dies in 2006 with an estate of $2 million, there will be a tax due of $780,800; the person also has a tax credit of $780,800. That person's estate will have no estate tax to pay, because the tax due is equal to the credit that's available.

The basic rule of gift and estate tax is that you pay tax calculated on both the gifts you make during life and the gifts you

---

[33]Many planners believe these numbers may change because of the costs of the war on terrorism, the war in Iraq and the costs of reconstruction of the Gulf area after the 2005 hurricanes. Watch the news!

make at death. You have a credit that you can use to offset the tax that is due from these gifts. We call this the **credit shelter amount**, **the tax free amount**, or **the exclusionary amount**.

There are several exceptions to the general gift and estate tax rule. You will read more detail about most of them in Chapter 10.

1. You can give any amount to your American spouse,[34] and that amount is deductible from the taxable estate. This is called the **Marital Deduction**. America's richest person can die tax-free if he/she leaves all the assets to a spouse. This gift brings its own problems, because it burdens the surviving spouse's estate with ownership of all the money that was owned by both spouses. But using the marital deduction eliminates a tax on the first partner's death.

2. You can give up to $12,000 to any number of people each year [35]. Your spouse can also. If you go to the church one Sunday, and give a $12,000 check to each person who arrives, even if it adds up to a million dollars, there will be no tax on those gifts. This is called the **annual exclusion amount**.

3. You can give away up to $1milllion before death and it will be a deduction from the exclusionary amount. It doesn't need to be all in one gift. Your credit on the gift will be applied, so no tax will be due at the time of the gift. This amount is in addition to the annual exclusionary amount that you are allowed to give each year. Read more about this in Chapter 10.

4. You can give money in any amount to schools for tuition

---

[34]See Chapter 16 for a discussion of the marital deduction for foreign spouses.
[35]This used to be $10,000 but it must be adjusted each year, to the nearest $1,000. In 2002, it was adjusted to $11,000 and in 2006 it was adjusted to $12,000.

and to health care providers for services for the benefit of other people. It will not count against your credit shelter amount, and it is not limited by the $12,000 gift rule. You just have to make the check payable to the school or to the health care provider. Do not write the check to Grandma for her doctor bill; write it directly to the doctor. Read more about this in Chapter 10.

5. You have a benefit called the **stepped-up basis**.[36] When you die, the government is going to tax your estate on the current fair market value of everything you owned at the moment of death. Since you are taxed at that value (instead of the amount you paid), it is only fair that your heirs shouldn't have to pay capital gains tax in addition, if they sell the property after your death. Your estate may have to pay the death tax, but your heirs do not have to pay any capital gains on what they inherit. Again, this is detailed in Chapter 10.

6. You can give unlimited amounts to tax-free entities like charitable institutions (the hospital or religious organizations) or civic organizations (the community theater) and there will be a deduction from the taxable estate.

The rest of this chapter will concentrate on the Credit Shelter Trust.

The Credit Shelter Trust

First let's look at the basic plan for reducing the tax on a married couple's estate, using the Credit Shelter Trust.

Suppose a couple has a $5 million estate. Each owns half of the estate. The husband dies in 2006 and leaves his half to his wife. There

---

[36]Watch for changes in the stepped-up basis. After 2010, if the 2001 tax bill is ratified, this becomes the new way to calculate the replacement for the estate tax. More detail in a later chapter.

is no tax due because of the unlimited marital deduction. Then in 2008 she dies.[37] Now she has a $5 million estate. When she dies in 2008, she leaves $2 million tax-free but the remaining $3 million is taxed at the marginal rate of 45%.[38] Here is how the result looks:

$5 million estate (wife's and husband's combined at her death)
Tax is calculated this way:

$2,130,000 total tentative[39] tax due in 2008
- 780,800 credit against tax in 2008[40]
$1,350,000 total tax due

$5,000,000 estate
-1,350,000 total tax due
$3,650,000 remaining for the children

---

[37] I am leaving out a calculation for this discussion. In reality, when two people die within a short time of each other (the second one inheriting from the first to die), there is an additional credit against the tax. If I added that calculation here, it would be confusing.

[38] The difference between the tax-free amount and the available credit is a little confusing. For discussion purposes, it is easier to talk about the tax-free amount. But that's not really how we calculate the final tax. In the examples I've given, you will see the credit amount deducted, not the tax-free amount. In this example, the tax free amount is $2 million. We calculate the initial tax due (the tentative tax), then we subtract the tax credit that is available for $2 million (the $780,000 credit).

[39] The tentative tax is the first calculation, before we deduct the credit.

[40] $780,000 is the credit available for the $2 million the decedent owned

Suppose this couple wrote Wills, *not* leaving all their money to each other outright (each will says the same thing), like this:

"I'd like to give all my money to my wife, but then at the end, she would have to pay too much tax. So instead, I will take the credit shelter amount, and I will put it into a trust. I will not give that money to my wife. The trustee of the trust will give my wife all the income. If she needs any of the principal because there is not enough of her own money, then the trustee can give out principal too. When she dies, the remaining money goes to our children. My wife does not own the money, so it's not included in her estate for tax purposes."

The only restriction on this plan is that the money paid out of the principal has to go for health, education, maintenance, and support -- not for luxuries. No year-long trips on the Queen Mary, no Porsche. Just health, education, maintenance, and support. Here is the best part: Wife gets to be the trustee. The wife is really playing two roles: she is both the trustee and the beneficiary. So, the surviving wife can manage the money and can decide how much principal to give herself, if any. She has a duty to care for the beneficiary (herself) and to preserve the funds which are not needed by the beneficiary for the final heirs, i.e., the children (they are also referred to as The Remaindermen).

Using a Credit Shelter Trust

Now let's use the same figures, using a Credit Shelter Trust.[41] When the husband dies, the result is different: Now, out of his $2.5 million (his half of the estate) he puts $2 million into the trust. Then he gives his wife the rest or $500,000. Her estate now has $3 million (that

---

[41]The Credit Shelter Trust is also called the *Equivalency Trust*, the *Bypass Trust*, and the *AB Trust*. The name used depends on where you live.

is, her own $2.5 million -- half of what they had together -- plus the $500,000 the husband left her). You should recognize that the husband has no tax due on his estate because the first $2 million was tax free under the credit shelter rule and the next $500,000 was tax free because he left it to his wife. So we have no tax calculation for the husband.

What is the tax result, and what is left for the children when she dies in 2008? Compare this calculation to the earlier one:

$3,000,000, wife's estate:

$1,230,800 tentative taxes due
-    780,800 credit amount
  $450,000 total tax due

$3,000.000 estate
- 450,000 tax due
$2,550,000 for the children from wife's estate

The children will obviously prefer this approach because the money in the Credit Shelter Trust from the husband will pass to the children, tax-free at wife's death:

$2,000,000 from husband's Credit Shelter Trust
$2,550,000 from wife's estate (after estate tax)
 $4,550,000 total

That is a much better result than the first scenario, where the husband left everything to the wife, rather than in a trust. By putting the husband's tax-free amount into a trust, it was never taxed when he died and it was never taxed when the wife died. The difference is a tax-savings of $900,000!

You are probably wondering whether anyone is monitoring the wife. Nobody is watching her, at least not right away. Ultimately, the children and the IRS will be watching.

Here is an example:

Wife gives herself all the income each year. This gives her enough income to live on, along with her social security and her pension. But over time, the money doesn't go as far. The stock market is down, and she has had heavy medical bills. Her own investments have lost money. She used to work, but now she is at retirement age. And the car wears out. Now she either needs $20,000 for a new car, or an additional $450 per month for a car payment. This is a reasonable distribution of the principal for maintenance. She needs a car and she does not have enough of her own money to buy one. No one can complain.

Let's change the story:

The wife has $1 million of her own; it is invested and producing $80,000 in yearly income. She hasn't had any unusual health care expenses. The trust has the same amount, and she gets all that income too; so her income totals $160,000. Her life is going fabulously. She wants a new car. She doesn't really need the trust to pay out of the principal; she just doesn't want to spend her own money. The children may complain if she uses trust funds to pay for the car since that money is going to be theirs when she dies. She does not have the right to squander it.

Here is the rule: if you are minding the cookie jar, you must keep your hands out of the cookie jar unless there is nothing else to eat! You may not make principal distributions from the Credit Shelter Trust unless there is no reasonable way to the get capital anywhere else.

The Credit Shelter Trust is the basic building block of estate planning. It is legal, and it is often used. Remember that the goal is not to deprive your spouse; it is to make sure the surviving spouse has the use of the money and control of the money but not the taxable ownership of the money when he or she dies.

A Variation: the Disclaimer Credit Shelter Trust

Many of my clients have the possibility of estate tax issues, but with the shifting tax code amount, they may not have to face tax issues. Life is always changing: their stocks went up, they got a promotion, they lost a great job, health problems took up their savings. Perhaps I should create a Credit Shelter Trust in their Wills, but if they don't need a trust when one partner passes, the survivor will be upset that he/she has to deal with it. Maybe I should advise them to avoid the trust for now, and come back later if their finances escalate. But what if the money rises and they don't come back to see me? Three years later, there's a tax issue and the survivor is furious with me for not putting the trust in place.

The solution is to create the Disclaimer Credit Shelter Trust. The Will leaves everything to the spouse, with the flexibility to choose a trust or not:

> "I leave everything to my wife. If she disclaims any portion, then that portion shall be given to the trustee of my Credit Shelter Trust."

The spouse has nine months to make the Disclaimer. I use this plan for many clients. Some planners don't like to use the Disclaimer Credit Shelter Trust, because a despondent surviving spouse may miss the nine month deadline, or might break one of the disclaimer rules. In my opinion, until the estate tax code is ratified, it's the safest choice.[42]

---

[42]If you are worried about your spouse's next partner, then you better use the Credit Shelter Trust. That's the safest way to make sure the kids get the money!

Chapter 10: Gifts - Tax-Free Exclusions

Gifting

Yearly Gifting

Some gifts are so small that the government cannot be bothered keeping track. You do not have to pay tax on a gift of $12,000 or less.[43] You can make the gift to anyone, anywhere, and you can make as many of these gifts as you like. Your spouse can do the same. It will not reduce your credit shelter amount.

In any year that you make a gift that is larger than $12,000, you must report the gift on a special gift tax form by April 15; any amount you give over $12,000 reduces the credit shelter amount. The gift has to be completed -- meaning you have to deliver the money. It cannot be a promise or a deposit into an account that cannot be touched until some condition is met, such as finishing school.[44]

One of the ways to reduce estate taxes is to make an estate smaller by giving money away every year. This is not a technique for the young: you still might need our money and it may be too early to give it away!

Imagine this situation:

Grandma is 86 in 2006, has been widowed, has had a stroke, is frail, and her family history tells her that she probably won't

---

[43]Remember, this is adjusted yearly for inflation, to the $1,000 level. It used to be $10,000 and in 2006, it increased to $12,000.

[44]I am ignoring certain realities. Some state rules do not allow individuals under age 18 to own large amounts of money. There are also some exceptions, such as the Crummey Trust, described in Chapter 3.

live more than four years. Let's presume she will die in 2009, so she has the opportunity to make gifts for four years. If she has a big estate (let's say $4.5 million), she needs to start reducing her assets because every dollar that she owns above the credit shelter amount will be taxed between 35%-45% in 2009. If she has three children and seven grandchildren, she can give away $12,000 to each one, without a gift tax ($120,000) each year. She decides to give each child and grandchild $12,000 on each January 1, starting in 2006. At that rate, she can reduce her estate by $480,000. In 2009, when she passes away, her estate is reduced to $4,020,000. If she made the gifts, then her estate tax would be $929,200 and if she didn't make the gifts, then her estate tax would be $1,150,000. The family members enjoy an additional $220,800 in tax savings because she made the gifts prior to death, in the tax free amounts.

Joint Gifting

A married person can make the gift equal to double the tax free amount, even if only one of the couple is making the gift. One of the partners might make a gift alone because he or she has separate funds that are not owned by both of them (for instance, money from an inheritance or money earned before marriage). The gift does not have to come from community property or jointly owned property. The spouse with the funds makes the gift for $24,000[45] ($12,000 for each one) on behalf of both spouses and reports it to the IRS at the end of the year, using a benefit called *gift splitting*. As long as one spouse can make the gift for both, the gift amount can be double the tax free amount that would ordinarily be allowed for one of them.

---

[45] Or whatever the amount of the tax free gift is that year.

Educational or Health Care Gift

You can also make a gift on behalf of anyone for any amount, as long as the money is for educational tuition or health care. It is important to remember that you must send the money directly to the institution or to the health care provider. If niece gets the check, then it is a gift to her. If niece's school gets the check directly to pay tuition, the amount in excess of $12,000 is not treated as a taxable gift or as a reduction of the credit shelter amount.

Why would the government let you do this? Remember that tax policy serves two purposes: one is to raise money and the other is to motivate people to act in socially acceptable ways. Spending your money to pay for someone else's education or health care, when they are in need, reduces requests for government funding. It is an activity the government wants to reward.

Examples

Let's look at a few examples of these different tax applications we have considered so far:

- You and your spouse want to help your niece with her new business. You send her a check for $20,000 from your joint checking account as a gift. There is no gift tax, because each of you is entitled to make a gift of $12,000 tax-free, or $24,000 (in 2006).

- You and your spouse want to help the same niece, but she needs $30,000. You send the check from your joint checking account. Each of you makes a $12,000 tax-free gift. The additional $6,000 must be reported by each of you when you file your income tax, using the gift tax form. You each made a taxable gift of $3,000. The $3,000 is deducted from the credit shelter amount allowed to each of you.

79

- You and your spouse want to help pay for the birth of your grandchild, who was born prematurely without adequate insurance. You send a check in the amount of $32,000 to the hospital to cover the uninsured part of the bill. There is no need to treat this as a gift limited to the $12,000 amount, because you paid the hospital directly.

- Husband has a significant inheritance and his new wife has no personal funds. They both want to give her mother money for home improvement. He gives her mother $20,000 and there is no gift tax even though it's his separate inheritance money. They report the gift on their tax return and claim it as a split gift. It doesn't matter that the gift came only from the husband's money. It is fully allowable and there is no reduction in the gift exclusion amount for either one of them.

The Stepped-up Basis - The Only Gift from the IRS!

Basis refers to the cost we pay for something. For a business item, the basis is reduced for wear and tear, which is depreciation, but increased for improvements. When assessing the value of an asset, we also have to take into account inflation and the current fair market value. We live with inflation, and things often are worth more than we paid for them. Think of your home: Whatever it cost, it is probably worth much more now than what you paid.

At the moment of your death, everything must be valued at the *fair market value* for estate tax purposes. We will use that figure to determine your estate tax. So, at death, your heirs get a break. Since the asset is included in your taxable estate at its fair market value, your heirs get to use fair market value as the new *basis* when it is sold. When they sell it, they don't have to pay capital gains tax on the difference between the purchase price and the value at the date of your death. This is true, even if the estate is not large enough to attract a tax that exceeds the credit shelter amount.

Here's an example:

Dad paid $50,000 in 1980 for his business building. When he died in 2008, it was worth $450,000. He didn't have a taxable estate because his assets didn't total $2 million. If Dad sold the building the day before he died, then he would have to pay taxes based on the increase in value in his income tax for that year. We calculate the tax due using the difference between the sale price and the purchase price: $450,000 sale price minus $50,000 basis = $400,000 gain x 15% capital gains tax rate which equals $60,000.

Try this sale a different way:

Dad didn't sell the building; instead, he owned it when he passed away. He owes no estate tax. His heirs sold the building, but for purposes of calculating their capital gains, there is zero tax. That is because the basis is the fair market value at his death that has *stepped up* from $50,000 to $450,000. So, the sale price ($450,000) minus the purchase price or cost basis ($450,000) equals zero capital gains. The heirs are $60,000 richer because Dad owned the building at the time of his death. This result happens even though there is no estate tax due!

Comparison:

$450,000 fair market value	$450,000 fair market value
- 50,000 cost basis	$450,000 cost basis
400,000 capital gains	0 capital gains
x 15% tax rate	
$ 60,000 capital gains tax	$0 tax

Pay attention to this rule! It may not be wise to sell something to clean up the estate or make it simpler for your heirs. The Step-Up applies to both halves of the community property if you live in a community property state. Check out any potential sale with an accountant or an attorney to see if it makes any difference in the estate tax or income tax.

The Step Up in Basis is just about the only gift you are ever going to get from the IRS.[46] Under the new tax law, after 2010, it is the foundation for the new form of estate tax. So, watch this area closely. This may change as Congress reviews whether to ratify the 2001 tax bill as it was passed or whether to do something else with *basis*. (See Chapter 14 on the new tax bill.)

Gifting Large Amounts of Money

Some of my clients are extremely blessed. They could give away the whole credit shelter amount, and they would still have plenty of money. Let's presume that the price of everything is going up. Housing is booming, stocks are rising, and so they continue to make money. If he or she holds on to everything until death, appreciation will probably make it worth more tomorrow than today, and that increases the tax amount that will be due. So, this person makes the courageous decision to give away the full amount of the credit shelter amount now.

Consider this situation:

In 2007, widowed Dad is 58 years old with assets of $4 million. He has four children, age 24 to 32. All have young families with

---

[46] The Stepped-Up Basis does not apply to gifts made during life! So if you transfer a stock with a basis of $5,000 during your lifetime, then the person who receives it will have income tax due on the difference between the sales price and the $5,000 basis, when it is sold. When this happens, it is called the "transferred basis".

small children. They work hard, don't squander their money, and they pay their bills, but they just aren't getting ahead. It will take years of saving before they can afford to move from their small houses to what they really need to raise their growing families. Since the price of housing is rising faster than inflation, it will always be a challenge to purchase a larger home. Dad decides to give $250,000 to each one to buy a house. The value to the children is obvious: they get a new house right now.

After making the gift, Dad's estate is growing more slowly and that's just what he wants. When the father dies, he has $1 million less in his estate. If he had kept the $1 million and lived to 2009, that money would have grown. In other words, there would have been a taxable increase in his estate if he didn't make the gift, and Dad simply decided the growth would be on his children's side of the ledger, not on his. There may eventually be a tax due on this growth, but it will be at his children's deaths, not his. This is one of the primary rules of tax planning: delayed tax is usually better! This choice isn't for everyone, but for those who have more than enough, and see their wealth increasing, this is a choice to consider.

Gifting on the Day of Death

More than once, a client has contacted me, knowing death is at the door. If it is the last thing he does, he is determined to deprive Uncle Sam of the estate tax. So, at that moment when he might otherwise be saying his final goodbyes, he is writing checks and transferring cash! These are the people who know that they are in the highest tax bracket for estate tax, and every dollar given to a grandchild before death is about 45 cents that Uncle Sam doesn't get.

You may not want to spend your last moments this way, but it does have value for those who chose it. It is not a good plan for a few reasons. Your last moments should be spent saying *"I love you"* to the people that count and remembering the best that life gave you and recalling the best you gave to life. This is also a good time to remind your Creator about all the good things you did. Don't waste this moment of opportunity thinking about taxes! You might not be alert enough to give away money at the last moment. Pain and drugs tend to clog up your thinking. And, it is better to have a gifting plan over a period of time if there's a lot to give away.

But having said all that, let me give you another version of this story:

The dying Client never gave away a dime before now, has no intention of doing it, and figures they can all get whatever is left when he is gone. He'll be damned if he'll pay any lawyer to talk him into giving away his money while he still needs it. He has made lots of money, and the lawyer probably hasn't, so what could the lawyer know? After all, he is only 93, the cancer isn't spreading very fast, and he may need that $5 million when he gets better. Those youngsters just don't appreciate the value of money and they'll just squander it on something useless. And besides (he thinks this is the most logical answer of all), gifting is for the rich, and he is not rich! So forget about gifting during his life, he huffs and puffs. And then he slips into a coma. The doctor tells his son that the angel of death is on his way. The son has a Power of Attorney, and that document lets him give away money if it improves Grandpa's tax situation. Cold-hearted as it seems, the son now has a dilemma. If he gives away the money right after Grandpa went to sleep, it seems like all he is thinking about is the money. But if he doesn't give away some money, then everything that Grandpa still has in his own accounts will be taxed at nearly 46%. What's a good son to do? I cannot tell you what he should do. It is a personal decision.

Here is *how* he should do it if he decides to give away the money. Here are the rules:

- The money has to be out of Grandpa's account before he dies.[47]

- If he is dying in the next few hours, a check is out of the question. It will take days to go through the bank's clearing house.

- You have to use cash or a cashier's check. Someone has to go to the bank, get cash or cashier's checks, and deposit them directly into the childrens' accounts (or do wire transfers) or hand-deliver the cash or cashier's check.

This is a lot of work. You could be robbed of the cash in the parking lot. The other children probably haven't told their brother their bank account numbers. In short, the last hours will be spent frantically doing everything except saying a loving goodbye. Try to avoid this final scene. Try to plan for this at least a few days (months, years) ahead. Better yet, try to get Grandpa to talk with a financial planner or lawyer long before this date comes.

---

[47] Ask your tax planner or attorney before you take money out of accounts that are joint tenancy with the right of survival! This is a tricky area that can cause a lot of grief! Again, you can make mistakes if you try to do this in the last moments.

Chapter 11: Charitable Gifts

Charitable Gifting at Death

When a taxpayer passes away, and the government takes estate tax, the money goes into the general fund. The taxpayer does not get to decide how the money is spent. Congress has made that choice through its funding bills. If someone asked you where you would like to see that money spent, you could come up with some good ideas of your own.

Perhaps you always wanted to give a scholarship to the school you attended. Maybe you appreciated the non-profit drug treatment agency that turned your nephew's life around. Your church or synagogue may need a social hall. Your list could get long.

It may surprise you that you can make a choice about where your estate tax money goes. You can use your Will or your Living Trust to give the money to a tax-free organization and have it deducted from your taxable estate. Your heirs will not get the money, but you get the satisfaction of knowing that while you could not avoid the estate tax laws, at least you were able to choose how the money is spent on social needs.

I want to leave with you one more idea. Your Will or your Living Trust is your final statement of how you want your money used. You will not get another chance to do a good deed! Either do it during your life, or do it through your Will or Living Trust. This is your last chance. Even a small gift means a lot to the Boy Scouts, or the library or the Children's Hospital fund. Those small gifts are always appreciated, and your heirs probably won't miss the money. They may even be proud of you!

Charitable Gifting during Life

Why not make the donation during your life? Suppose you have a modest estate and you would like to give to charity right now. Yet, you are concerned that if you give too much, you won't have enough to care for yourself. There is a solution.

How would you like to sell your stocks, take the profits free from paying capital gains, reinvest the money to pay yourself a higher dividend, and get a charitable deduction too? Sounds too good to be true, but true it is. There is a way to accomplish all those things using one of the Charitable Remainder Trusts, which I will describe later. These trusts are not right for everybody, but for some people, they are a wonderful opportunity. They are legal and well regarded.

Most churches and universities can help you plan for this type of arrangement. The IRS offers guidance on how to accomplish good results. Think back to one of the goals of tax law: getting you to act in socially appropriate ways. If the IRS makes it easy for you to give to a charity, then you are more likely to do it.

The usual way to do this is to create a trust and contribute some assets -- whether cash, stocks, or land. The trust pays you an income for a term of years or for your entire life, if that is what you want. At the end of your term or life, the charity gets the money in the trust. This meets your need for income during your life and gives you a current income tax deduction for the charitable contribution (even though the charity doesn't get the money until some time in the future). It also gives you the satisfaction of helping a charity.

Take Advantage of the Charity's Tax-Free Status

Here's an added bonus: You may get more income from the assets in the trust than you would if you kept the stock yourself because a charity does not have to pay income tax. This example shows how you get more income from the trust assets than you could on your own:

1. Suppose you have stock that you inherited from your father. Initially, it was worth $10 per share when you inherited it. And 25 years later, it is selling for $50 per share. But the stocks are not paying healthy dividends. You need to sell some of the stock in order to purchase securities that pay better dividends. You could sell the stock but then you personally pay capital gains tax on the $40 gain when you sell. At 15% tax, you lose $6, and you have only $44 to reinvest.

2. If instead, you contribute the inherited stock to the charitable trust, and the trust sells it (to purchase a stock that pays more income), there is no income tax on the $40 of gain because the charitable trust is tax-free. Now the trust can reinvest the entire $50 in a stock that pays more income. You get the income on the $50 investment from the trust during your lifetime, and afterwards the charity gets the stock.

If this type of arrangement suits you, then study the next examples of the specific types of charitable trusts: the Charitable Remainder Trust, the Charitable Remainder Unitrust, the Charitable Lead Trust, and the Charitable Gift Annuity. If not, then skip the next section.

Types of Remainder Trusts

There are two kinds of charitable remainder trusts: the **Charitable Remainder Unitrust (CRUT)** and the **Charitable Remainder Annuity Trust (CRAT)**. Both are worth considering, but one may better suit your risk tolerance than the other.

Charitable Remainder Unitrust

The **Charitable Remainder Unitrust (CRUT)** works like this:

1.   Mom and Dad, age 65, put $600,000 into a charitable remainder trust for their church in the year 2002. The taxpayer can make additional contributions to the trust later on.

2.   The trust invests the money so it produces income each year.

3.   Mom and Dad get an income from the trust for their lives, based on a percentage of the value of the trust assets.

4.   Mom and Dad receive the same percentage each year but the trust assets are valued yearly, and the value of the trust assets will vary. Mom and Dad chose the percentage rate when they set up the trust and they cannot change it. At 7%, the income is $42,000 per year, if the value of the trust assets remains $600,000. If the assets increase in value, they will get 7% of the new value.

5.   Mom and Dad get a tax deduction in the year they made the gift. The deduction is only for a part of the money they put into the trust: $144,336 (the present value of the remainder interest).[48] They can carry over the amount of the charitable

_____

[48]They cannot deduct the full $600,000 at the time of the creation of the trust, because they will continue to receive the income from the

contribution that they cannot use in any year.

If the trust has great investments, they will get more income. Of course, the income is taxable, but it would have been taxable if they had simply put it in the brokerage account. At the end of their lives, the money goes to the charity. The **CRUT** is a good choice for people who want their income to keep pace with the changing economy.

Charitable Remainder Annuity Trust

The **Charitable Remainder Annuity Trust (CRAT)** works almost the same way, but the annual income remains the same.

1. The donors get a set percentage of the initial value of the contribution. So, if they contribute $600,000 into a CRAT and want a 7% return, they will always get $42,000 per year, whether the trust earns more or less than that.

2. If there isn't enough income in a year, the trust has to pay some money out of the principal.

3. Using the same figures as the previous example for our calculation, this gives Mom and Dad an income tax deduction of $125,950. It is a lower deduction than with the CRUT, but the retirees have the security of knowing that the same payment will always be made, in good and bad times.

4. The taxpayer cannot make any additional gifts into this trust because the return is a fixed percentage of the original contribution.

The **CRAT** is a good choice for individuals who want the security of an income with a specific dollar amount they can count on,

annuity for their lifetimes. Their deduction will be calculated using an estimate of the number of years they are expected to live.

no matter what happens to the market.

Instead of a Trust, use The Charitable Gift Annuity

Maybe you don't want the bother of creating a trust and managing it as the trustee. You just want to give the money to a charity, collect your quarterly income checks, and get an income tax deduction. There is another option that works equally well. This is the **Charitable Gift Annuity**. The taxpayer gives the money to the charity. The charity creates an annuity that guarantees to pay an income over the taxpayer's lifetime. The taxpayer gets an immediate income tax deduction for the *present value of the remainder* (the actual current value of the amount that the charity will get when the taxpayer dies). Then the taxpayer gets the annuity payment for life or for a specific number of years. The amount the taxpayer gets depends on:

* the rate of interest being paid at the time the
   charity created the annuity,
* the age of the taxpayer,
* the length of payment period, and
* the start date of payments.

If a taxpayer donates at age 50 but does not want to collect any annuity payments until age 65, there will be a build up of earnings. The payments that can be made at age 65 will be larger than the payments that would begin at age 50.

The charity guarantees these payments. There is a safety feature: a charitable organization cannot offer these annuity plans unless they have been approved by the state. These plans are well managed and highly monitored by the state, so you should not have to worry about the safety of your money.

The money that the taxpayer receives yearly is treated differently for income tax purposes than it would be in the Charitable Remainder Trust. The taxpayer has actually purchased an annuity, through the charity. So, the income is taxed like any other annuity. Part of what you get with each check is a return of your investment, and part of it is a dividend or interest payment. You will get a tax statement from the charity, telling you which part of the payment is included in your income.

Usually there is an increase in cash flow when a Charitable Gift Annuity is purchased. That is because the charity can sell low basis assets and not pay any capital gains. Those assets can be reinvested in assets that pay a higher return. And part of the income the taxpayer gets each quarter is a return of capital, which is not taxed. So there is generally more income and less income tax. A great combination! The usual age for making the Charitable Gift Annuity is 65 to 70.

There are varieties of these types of plans. Universities, churches, synagogues, hospitals -- all kinds of charitable groups -- have development offices that will help you find a plan that works for you, if you are inclined to this kind of giving. And often, they have a list of attorneys who know how to handle this type of work.

Chapter 12: Advanced Estate Planning Techniques

If you've done the basic estate planning (like the Credit Shelter Trust, taking best advantage of the Stepped Up Basis, and maximum gifting each year), and if you still have an estate tax concern, more advanced techniques are available. The goal is to give away as much as possible, without lowering your lifestyle. You can have a good life; yet, at the time of death, you own less and pay less estate tax.

Remember that some of these techniques will still be valuable when the new tax code applies, and some won't. (The new tax code is discussed in chapter 14.)

This information gives you a taste of the opportunities that are available today. Each technique is described briefly. If you are interested in any one of them, you should consult a planning expert for the details of each one.

The House Trust

The *House Trust* is properly called the **Qualified Personal Residence Trust** (QPRT). Seniors love this technique if they've given away all that they can each year, or their heirs have enough money so that the $12,000 gift (the exclusionary amount) isn't meaningful. This technique literally gives away the house while you keep it. This technique is for people who have so much money that they must give it away; the benefits are not necessarily obvious.

Here's how it works: The residence of the taxpayer is put into a trust. The trust terms state that the taxpayer may live in the house for a specified number of years. The taxpayer has to make a good guess at how long he or she will live, because the trust has to end before the taxpayer dies. After that, the taxpayer cannot live there anymore unless he or she pays rent. The heirs then own the house. At the time the house is contributed to the trust, its value is divided into two parts. There is the value of living there for the taxpayer's term (whatever number of years the taxpayer says he will live there), and the remainder value (the value of the house for its expected life after the trust ends). We discount the value of the gift going into the trust. The taxpayer isn't giving away the full value of the residence, because he or she still gets to use it. Thus the discount - based on these factors:

- the age of the taxpayer
- how long the taxpayer has the use of the residence
- the current interest rate.

Say that the 68-year old taxpayer keeps the right to live in the house for five years, and then after that, the house belongs to the beneficiaries. The house has a current value of $400,000. There is a discount rate based on the current interest rate and the tables set up by the IRS. So after the discount, the gift value is $259,984. The taxpayer reports this as a taxable gift and here's the first gain: a house that was worth $400,000 has been given away but the taxpayer didn't have to use $400,000 of his credit shelter amount. He only used $259,984.

Remember that our taxpayer has too much money, and needs to transfer it to the heirs. The goal is for our taxpayer to continue a great lifestyle and to die owning as little as possible. But his term of years on using the home is up. He has either to move out or to pay rent to the heirs. Why is that a good deal for him? Because he now has an excuse to transfer money to the children. It is not a gift; it is rent. Yes, it's true that the heirs have an income tax associated with the money they are receiving, but they won't have to pay any estate tax on the value of the home. At the end of the five-year term, if the house appreciated at 4% interest, then the house value transferred to the heirs is worth $486,661, and the taxpayer only had a taxable gift of $259,984, *plus,* he gives them money each month as rent. It is a sweet deal.

This technique is only good for some people. You should have already used most of the other available simple techniques before using the QPRT. You should probably have a short-term expectancy to use the house without cost, and you should be willing to pay rent when the term is up. If you don't live for the amount of time you said you'd use the house while it was in the trust, then the whole plan collapses and the value of the house is included in your estate. It is a wonderful tool for the right people. Young people shouldn't do this.

The Grantor Retained Annuity Trust

The **Grantor Retained Annuity Trust** (GRAT) is an opportunity whose value taxpayers don't always appreciate, so they often need a planner to nudge them into this one. The taxpayer transfers funds to the trust now, but he gets the income from the trust for a specified period of years. There is a gift tax but, like the QPRT we just considered, the value of the trust is divided into two parts.

One part is the value of the earned income, which the grantor keeps, and one part is the value of the money that the beneficiary gets later. Like the QPRT, there is a discount on the gift, because the beneficiary doesn't get the whole gift at once. At the time of creating the trust, the taxpayer chooses whether to take a fixed dollar amount of income each year or to take a fixed percentage of the trusts assets valued at the time the trust is created.

Here's an example:

Mr. T contributes $100,000 to a grantor-retained trust when he is 65 years old for the benefit of his friend (the beneficiary). He gets the quarterly income at 6% interest for a term of 10 years, or $6,000 per year. After that, the trust funds are not for his use, but for the benefit of his friend, the beneficiary. If he made the gift outright, he would be making a gift of $100,000 and he would have to pay gift tax on that amount. But using the Grantor Retained Trust, he is only making a gift of $45,011, which is the residual value after he uses the money for 10 years.

There are naturally some downsides to the GRAT. The main one is that it is a **grantor trust**. That means that, no matter how much income the grantor is getting, he or she has to pay tax on all the income of the trust. In this case, if the trust Mr. T created earns $8,000 in one year, he can only take the annuity distribution of $6,000 and the additional $2,000 will remain in the trust for the beneficiary. However, Mr. T must pay the income tax due on the full $8,000. While this may seem a downside, it depends on your perspective. If Mr. T has too much money and wants to leave it to someone else, this is an opportunity to use his own cash to pay the tax on someone else's money. And if you are desperately trying to move money away from yourself, this is a good thing.

The Grantor Retained Unitrust

The **Grantor Retained Unitrust** (GRUT) works in a similar way. The difference is that the grantor selects a percentage of the assets as his or her income interest. The assets are valued on the first day of each year, for a period of years. If the value of the trust goes up, the grantor gets a percentage of that amount instead of a percentage of the original amount, and so the income can keep pace with inflation.

If the goal is to keep pace with inflation until the gift is completely given to the beneficiary, this is the better choice of the grantor trusts. If the goal is to give as much as possible to the beneficiary, including the income tax costs of the growing trust, then the GRAT is the better choice. The GRAT and the GRUT will have different gift values. That is another consideration in choosing which one to use.

Family Partnership

No discussion of estate tax savings would be complete without a discussion of the Family Partnership. This method of owning a business has several advantages, but we will focus on the estate planning aspects. This business entity is easy to set up, and the owners (including the children who received shares in the partnership) share the income.

For instance:

Parents own an office building worth $800,000, and they give away a 2.5% interest to each of their two children. They have made a gift valued at $40,000 (5% of $800,000) or $10,000 from each parent to each child. This is a tax-free gift. The partnership agreement says the income will be divided among the partners proportionate to their share of ownership. If the building has a net income of $30,000, then the children should each have a share of that income of $750 (2.5%). If the partnership is liquidated, all the partners receive a proportional share of the asset value. Each child would receive 2.5% of the value. If the parent works in the business, then that person must be paid adequately for her services. In this example, the net income must include a payment to Dad for his services, before arriving at the partnership income of $30,000.

Signs of partnership

This brings us to the three major rules of partnership:

1. The capital must produce income. The capital in our example is the building. It produces rental income. What if the parents were a singing duo that did TV commercials, and they put that business activity into a partnership? Capital is not the income-producing factor; their personal services produce the income.

2. The partners must be real partners in interest. That means that each one must really have an ownership interest.

3. They each become personally liable for the debts if the partnership cannot pay them. (If you don't like this third requirement, see the Limited Partnership described below).

Assets owned by the partnership

Another advantage of the partnership is that the partnership (not the individual members of it) becomes the owner of real estate. This can be a real advantage if the property is located in a different state from where the individuals live. Suppose the partnership owns a building in one state and the partners live in another. If one partner dies in his home state, his interest in the partnership is included in his probate estate. Since he does not own property independently in the state where the property is located, his personal representative doesn't have to open a probate in the other state.

Discounting of values

The most widely advertised advantage of the partnership is the ability to discount the share given away, whether during life or at death. When family members hold a business and one family member owns a large share, then that share becomes less marketable. Anyone who buys into that arrangement must deal with the family members and the family politics. That is not the straightforward business arrangement one faces with stocks in Boeing or General Electric. The founder in a family business usually has some direct control, by the partnership agreement, but he also has emotional influence over the family member shareholders. An outsider may not want to pay the full price for a share of ownership. So, the IRS is willing to allow a discount on the value of the shares that are passed on.

Here's an example:

Dad started his own cookie company as a younger man. He has now run it his way for 30 years. He is a fantastic businessman, but set in his ways, domineering, and determined. He wants to transfer shares to his children. If the shares of the business were sold to the public, the book value, the earnings, the debt, and so on, would be considered. But this situation is not like dealing with PepsiCo, which has a professional board of directors and public accounting.

This is a family business. Dad hates to give dividends (unless he wants a new car that year). He makes all the decisions without consulting anyone. And he is grouchy and evasive if anyone questions him. Heaven forbid that someone should require an accounting or a justification!

No one in the public would pay the full price for a minority share of this company, knowing they have to deal with Dad. So when valuing the shares, there is a discount. You need a professional appraiser to calculate the discount. Depending on the circumstances, you might get a 30% to 50% discount. So, if Dad gives away shares that are otherwise valued at $100, they might be discounted to $70. That means he can give away more shares, before he uses up his $12,000 gift limit or his credit shelter amount.

This is not intended to be a full discussion of the topic of discounting. If the partnership qualifies under the rules for capital and ownership, the taxpayer can allow the children to take income from the partnership. This puts less money in the parent's pocket, which is a great opportunity if the parent already feels he or she has too much money. And the parent can transfer the ownership of the asset to the children at a value that is lower than expected.

Limited Partnership

There is a variation on this theme of Family Partnership. We use it when the parent isn't ready to give up full control of the business. A Limited Partnership is like the General Partnership discussed above except that the only thing that is transferred is the right to receive income of the partnership and the right to receive a share of the asset value at the time of liquidation, but it does not include the right to vote on partnership business. If retaining control of the business is one of the parent's goals, then the parent keeps General Partnership shares for herself and gives away Limited Partnership Interests.

The limited partners are not responsible for partnership debt either, except up to the value of their interest in the partnership. Their personal assets will never be at risk for partnership debt. Limited partnership shares are not as valuable as general shares, so the parent has to transfer more shares to maximize the full value of the $12,000 gift (the exclusionary amount) or the credit shelter amount. The lack of business control by younger members of the family makes this an attractive choice to some.

Chapter 13: The Generation Skipping Tax

Everybody wants to avoid taxes during life and when they pass on. And the people who have a great deal of money want to make sure that they avoid double taxation as money passes down the line to younger members. You are probably wondering how the money could be taxed twice. Here's how. Mary is a widow, with three children. She has substantial wealth, far above the tax exclusion amount. And her children are in a very healthy financial position as well. When she dies, she will leave them all her money. Suppose that Mary is 90 years old, and her children are 68, 66 and 64. Her grandchildren are twenty years younger than their parents. Now suppose that Mary leaves all her money to the children and they pass on, leaving their own money plus Mary's money to their own children. Mary's money is taxed when she dies and then its taxed again when her children die, leaving it to the grandchildren. Mary can avoid some tax if she will skip her children, and pass some of the funds directly to the grandchildren. So instead of leaving all the money to the children, she creates a Will which leaves some of it for the grandchildren. Now it is only taxed once, when she dies.

Congress has already anticipated this move! It's a good plan for Mary's family, but it has an effect on the Treasury. So Congress has passed the Generation Skipping Tax (GST). We can leave money to the younger generations tax free, but only a certain amount escapes the GST. Here's what you can leave to younger generations without incurring an additional tax:

2002	$1.1 million
2003	$1.1 million[49]
2004-2005	$1.5 million
2006, 2007, 2008	$2.0 million
2009	$3.5 million

---

[49]That year was adjusted for inflation.

The tax rate on the excess above the exempt amount declines from 55% in 2002 to 45% in 2007 and thereafter. Remember, this tax is in addition to the gift tax and the estate tax.

You can use your exemption amount either in life with gifts, or at death with inheritance, just like you use the gift and estate exemption amount. If you make a gift of the annual exclusion amount (see chapter one) then it's not deducted from the GST exemption. You can allocate the exemption in any way you want, over many gifts during different times; however, once the exemption is designated, it is irrevocable.

This is an extremely complicated area of estate tax law. The definitions and rules are not obvious. If you and your youngsters have sufficient funds to fit into this scenario, you need to see an estate planner to get the best advantage. Like the estate tax generally, the generation skipping tax is due to expire in 2010. And like the estate tax, that may not happen, depending on the way Congress chooses to act. If this tax affects your family, then be sure to check with your planner periodically.

Chapter 14: Changing Tax Rules

The Economic Growth and Tax Relief Reconciliation Act of 2001

You learned the current state of estate tax law in the previous chapters, so you have the basics. Now for the news...with the Economic Growth and Tax Relief Reconciliation Act of 2001 (EGTRRA), it is all supposed to change!

The changes in the gift and estate tax code were passed into law on June 6, 2001 (Public Law 107-16) and they are temporary. That's because Congress is not allowed to pass any budget resolution that will take effect more than ten years from the time of passing it, unless it is ratified later. Unless Congress acts to make the new law permanent, the changes described in this chapter are designed to go back to what the law was before 2010.

The political climate surrounding this issue, in 2006, is a raging storm, to say the least! The Republican party wants the estate tax completely repealed, but that seems unlikely. The Democratic party won't be able to keep the estate tax exactly as it is either. The current "word on the street" is that there will be a reduction in the estate tax, but that the agreement between the parties must be an estate tax bill that raises at least half of the revenue that we raised under the current system. If I had to offer my best guess, I would say that the estate tax of the future will apply to estates of $5 million or more, or $10 million for a married couple. Look for the new legislation sometime between 2007 and 2009.

Upcoming Changes

This chapter is a short summary of the changes as of September 2006. I'll give you the outline first, and then an example of how it works in real life. The issues we discussed in the earlier chapters continue through 2009. In 2010, the estate tax is repealed, and we will have a "carry-over" or "transferred" basis.[50] The person who inherits the property takes the same basis as the person who passed away. There is no step-up in basis that year. In 2011, there is a new form of tax upon death, consisting of a capital gains tax on the decedent's assets.

Credit shelter amounts increase

The credit shelter amount is increased through 2009. [51] The new tax-free amounts and the resulting credit shelter amounts are listed below:[52]

2002-2003:	$1 million tax-free,	$345,800 credit amount
2004-2005:	$1.5 million tax-free,	$555,800 credit amount
2006-2008:	$2 million tax-free,	$780,800 credit amount
2009:	$3.5 million tax-free,	$1,525,800 credit amount

Tax rates will be lower

The estate, gift, and generation-skipping tax rates are lower. The maximum rates are:

2003:	49%
2004:	48%
2005:	47%
2006:	46%
2007-2009:	45%

---

[50]See Chapter 9 regarding the Step Up in basis.
[51] IRS Code Section 2010(c)
[52] For a discussion of the difference between the "tax-free amount" and the "credit amount", please see footnote 6.

Estate and gift taxes are separated

The gift tax is retained but the estate and gift taxes are no longer unified, as they were before 2002.[53] In earlier years, you could give away the credit shelter amount, either during your life or at your death. The IRS added together the gifts made during life and the gifts at death, and charged them against your unified credit. Starting in 2002, the gift and estate taxes were no longer unified. You have a credit for $1 million in gifts, which can be applied against the amount of credit available at death. From 2002 through 2003, both were $1 million. But starting in 2004, we had a $1.5 million tax-free amount at death and only $1 million tax free in gifts. This separation in gift and death tax is new.

The step-up in cost basis will change

In 2010, the use of the unlimited and automatic step-up in basis at death will end.[54] All property transferred from the decedent to the heirs takes the transferor's cost basis, just as a gift transfer would.

Someone must pay the income tax on the gain when it is eventually sold. Either you or your heirs will pay the capital gains tax. Under the current rules, the value of the property at death becomes the new basis to the heirs.

Here is an example of the current rule:

---

[53] IRS Code Section 2505(a).
[54] IRS Code Section 1014(f).The Stepped-Up Basis is explained in Chapter 1.

If an item cost $10 when purchased, and it is sold for $50 the day before death, then the taxpayer has a gain of $40, on which his estate must pay tax (his estate will do it for him, since he probably died before he could pay the tax himself.) However, if he died owning the property which cost $10, it will be included in his estate at a fair market value of $50. The heirs get a new basis of $50, *even if there is no taxable estate*, so when they sell it there is no taxable gain,. But under the new tax bill, starting in 2010, the unlimited automatic step-up in basis at death is eliminated.

Starting in 2011, the person who died can increase the basis of assets, but only up to a specified amount, and it can be spread among the various assets and heirs. The rules are complicated, but I have listed them here so you have a complete reference. Here's how you figure out the new basis:

The estate can increase the basis[55] of the various assets, by $1.3 million.[56] This amount is also increased by these considerations:

- Any gift of property to a spouse can be adjusted upwards by $3 million.[57]

- The increase in basis of any property is limited to its fair market

---

[55] Under the new code, basis is defined as the adjusted basis of the decedent or the fair market value, so if the fair market value is less than the basis, the estate can use that value.

[56] This amount is increased by the following things (1) the capital loss carryover allowed by Sec. 1212 (b); (2) the net operating loss carryover allowed by Sec. 172 (a) and (3) the losses associated with the property acquired by the heir, if the property would have been sold before the deceased person's death

[57] IRS Code Section 1022(c)

value.[58]

- Both halves of the community property can get the basis increase.[59]

- All these adjustments will be increased for inflation.

Property acquired by gift or other transfer that was not made for fair market value is not eligible for any of the basis adjustments, if it was received during the three years before death.

Comparisons before and after 2010

The handling of the cost basis (and the "step up" in basis) is one of the biggest changes made to the estate tax code, so let me give you an example:

Ben, a single person, dies in 2008, leaving an estate of $3 million. He has a $2 million tax-free amount at death. His estate tax will be $450,000 (without considering any expenses of the estate, and assuming he made no charitable contributions or prior gifts and that he has a zero basis in his assets). This is how it is calculated:

$3,000,000 taxable estate
$1,230,800 tentative tax in 2008[60]
$ 780,800 unified credit amount in 2008
$ 450,000 tax due

---

[58] IRS Code Section 1022(d)(2)
[59] IRS Code Section 1022(d)(1)(B)(iv)
[60] The calculation is as follows:
$780,800 tax due on the first $2,000,000
$450,000 (45% of the amount over $2,000,000)

The basis of his assets all take a step up to the fair market value on the date of death. When the heirs sell the assets, they pay no capital gains tax.

If he dies in the year 2009, there will be no estate tax, because the credit shelter amount increases that year to $3.5 million. Again, the heirs pay no capital gains tax.

Now we will presume he died in 2011 with the same facts. In that year, there will be no estate tax, as we know it today. His estate ($3 million and his assets have a basis of zero) can take an adjustment allowing part of the property to have an increase to increase the basis to $1.3 million. The executor of his estate decides which assets get the step-up in basis and which assets stay at his original basis. Assume his heirs sell the property immediately. The property receiving the step-up in basis, up to $1,300,000, will be sold without any capital gains tax attached. However, the heirs who received the $1.7 million in assets that did not receive the step-up in basis must pay tax when they sell their share of the estate. At the current 15% capital gains rate, that means they will owe $255,000 in tax.

Most taxpayers won't have that kind of a result! That's because most taxpayers won't have all their property classified as zero-basis assets. Let's change Ben's story, so that he doesn't have zero-basis property. Once again, we presume that Ben dies in 2011. This time let's assume that he still has property worth $3 million but instead of a zero basis, he has $1.7 million cost basis. When he dies, his estate can increase the cost basis of his assets by $1.3 million. The new cost basis is $3 million and all of his assets now enjoy a basis that is equal to the fair market value on the date of death. If the property were sold the next day for $3 million, his heirs have no capital gains due to the step-up in basis. And there is no estate tax that year.

Planning tips

Considering that we have several years before the new tax code applies, keep these in mind as tips for your planning:

- Use the Disclaimer Credit Shelter Trust. It gives the maximum flexibility until we know if Congress will ratify the EGTRRA Using this trust, you are saying: "I leave everything to my spouse, but if my spouse doesn't accept the funds, then the money should go into the Credit Shelter Trust". If the surviving spouse sees that the inheritance will make his or her estate become taxable, then the smart thing to do is to reject the inheritance and let it fall into the trust. It is not included in the survivor's estate for tax purposes.

- Keep excellent records of cost basis. When (and if!) we switch to the estate tax that relies upon a step up in basis for some property to $1.3 million, your heirs will need records of what you paid, your improvements, and so on.

- Continue to use the Irrevocable Life Insurance Trusts. Plan to use the life insurance proceeds to fund the capital gains due after 2009.

Please be aware that you will need to review all of these rules again in the next few years. Very few estate planners believe this new tax code will fall into place in 2010 as it is currently written. At the time the bill was written, we had a Treasury that could handle the decrease in tax dollars that would occur. In 2006, as this book goes to print, there is a question of whether that is still true.[61]

---

[61]Once again, I remind you that Congress must ratify this tax bill before 2010. This book goes to press in November, 2006. Look for changes sometime between 2007 and 2009.

Part Three - Taking Care of Your Spouse

Chapter 15: **The Marital Trust**

Before the 1960's, divorce and remarriage were less common. But multiple marriages have become a social reality. Now as well as then, when a person remarries, he/she wants to provide for the new spouse during his/her surviving years. But there was a glitch in the 1960's. If the man left any money to the second wife when he died, then she could do whatever she wanted with the money after he was gone. [62]

She might give it to those unpleasant children from her first marriage. He had children of his own for whom he wanted to provide. The second wife might or might not remember his children kindly when she died (or maybe she would remember them unkindly and intentionally leave them out!). The solution was obvious: Leave the money in trust, for the second wife's care until her death. Then the remainder would go to his children.

But then there was the ever-annoying tax code to consider. To get the marital deduction from the estate tax in earlier days, he had to leave it to her outright. If he put it in trust, it wasn't a completed gift, so there was no marital deduction at his death for the money he left the second wife in trust. His estate had to pay tax on that money, even though it was for the wife, because she didn't have the full use of the money. He was in a tough spot. Either he had to leave her without support and give the money to his kids, or he had to trust her to leave something to his own children when she wrote her own will, after his death. It was more than nerve racking.

---

[62] Please forgive my sexist bias in this example! There was a time in recent history when women earned no money or little money. We have grown way past that! The example could apply to either gender.

There is a joke about why this problem was eventually solved. Congress wouldn't budge on the issue, until divorce became so socially acceptable that Congressmen had second wives! Suddenly the concept of the marital trust became very real to the members of Congress. Whether this joke is true or not, it does make sense.

Qualified Terminable Interest Property Trust

IRS Code Section 2056 (b)(7) was added to solve the problem. It allows a marital trust to have a full marital deduction from the taxable estate, as long as all the income goes to the surviving spouse, and to no one else.[63] The trustee can distribute as much principal as the trustee feels is appropriate. There is no tax on any principal distribution. After the spouse dies, the remainder is distributed to whomever the deceased selected (usually the children of the first marriage). The estate tax is due when the surviving spouse dies, so the spouse has the full use of the money during life. This is the *Qualified Terminable Interest Property Trust* (QTIP).

There are other reasons (than second spouses) for people to use the marital trust. People use them if they fear that the surviving spouse cannot handle money or will let a new spouse take control of it (convert it to their own use). I rarely meet a woman who cannot understand money, insurance, retirement, mortgages, and credit. But my colleagues in the family law bar tell stories of people with money whose second spouse took advantage of them. These widows and widowers are targets for the person who sees an easy way to get hold of money.

The receptionist at the front desk may have seemed dull when you had a wonderful spouse waiting at home. And the insurance agent may have appeared uninteresting when he was selling that car policy,

---

[63] The rules for the marital deduction are more detailed than what I've described here. The main point is that all the income must go to the surviving spouse.

before your husband died. But our perceptions shift temporarily during periods of grief.

There is a saying in my line of work: a good widowed man won't last a year after the wife is gone. The single women are watching and he'll be scooped up in no time at all. A single woman may not last much longer. And it is just a hop and a skip to the next step, which is letting the new spouse be a joint owner of the house, the accounts, and the boat. The new spouse may take advantage of the accounts, spend them, or simply die last and not take care of the children you left behind.

And there is one last concern: Retail Therapy. Shopping makes me happy on a good day; on a bad day, it works wonders. There is normal grief associated with losing a beloved spouse. More than one woeful widow bought everything in sight, trying hard to buy her way out of depression.

If this is an area of concern, then a marital trust is for you. If it is not a concern, then take it no further. Not everyone needs or wants this type of arrangement. Just remember it's available if you decide it meets your needs.

Use a Living Trust

And remember, as the surviving spouse, to consider setting up a Living Trust for your heirs when you are preparing for a second marriage.

Chapter 16: Estate Planning for Foreign Spouses

The tax code grants an unlimited deduction from the estate tax for any amount one leaves to a spouse (who is a United States citizen) at death. This isn't just based on generosity of the Congress; it is based partially in political wisdom and practical sense. Seniors are a large voting block and it would be upsetting to them if they had to pay tax on assets the surviving spouse earned jointly with the one who died.

From a practical point of view, the money earned during a lifetime should be available to support both spouses until both are gone. And except for the time value of money, there is no loss to the government. Either the survivor will spend the money, and circulate it in the current economy, or the survivor will die owning the money, and the IRS will tax it then. This is why Congress is willing to allow a full marital deduction.

As you read these words, you are picturing a midwestern couple who have grown old together, and who both die on their Kansas farm. Picture something different:

A young American male works for Microsoft, spends a year in Japan, and meets a charming local lady in the Japan office. He marries her. When they return to the U.S., he acquires $5 million in Microsoft stock grants. By the time they have their first child at 30, they are doing fine financially. But when he dies unexpectedly, she is 31 years old with a newborn baby and far from her family. She quickly concludes that she needs help raising this baby, and she won't get it in a nation of strangers. She is going home to her family. He probably wrote a Will leaving everything to her. Ah, the tax man cometh in this case. Remember that a marital deduction is allowed based upon the belief that the survivor will spend the money in the U.S. or she will die in the U.S., where we plan to tax it when she dies. But she is moving away! She is a Japanese citizen. The United

States has no jurisdiction over her once she leaves, and she is free to take her share of the money as well as her husband's share. The United States would lose a bundle of tax money if a marital deduction were allowed.

You cannot use the marital deduction if you leave the money to a spouse who is not a U.S. citizen unless you follow certain rules that I will discuss next.

Qualified Domestic Trust

The solution requires that you write a valid Will or Living Trust. The basic rule is that, at your death, the money must go into a marital trust, discussed in an earlier chapter. But there are a few added rules:

- The spouse must get all the income.

- There must be at least one trustee who is a U.S. citizen.

- The trustee must be a bank if the assets in the trust are over $2 million (or if not a bank, then the trustee has some strict rules about securing the potential tax).

- Any time there is a distribution of capital, the trustee must pay the estate tax that would have been due on that money at the time of death.

Naturally, there are additional complex rules. The rules I've listed give you the outline. This is called the *Qualified Domestic Trust* (QDOT). There is some tax because whenever there is a principal distribution from the trust, tax is due. This differs from the Qualified Terminable Interest Property Trust for an American spouse, because the QTIP trustee can distribute the principal to the surviving spouse without paying any tax.

There is one other solution to the whole problem: become an American citizen. However, it often means that the foreign citizen must give up the citizenship of their birth. This doesn't appeal to everyone, and it has political and familial implications. I never recommend that someone change citizenship solely to avoid estate tax.

Chapter 17: Prenuptial and Living Together Agreements

Today, it is very common for couples to enter into agreements about their financial lives before they marry or begin living together. In most states, the courts accept the written agreements. The couples just have to follow some basic rules. Each partner fully discloses what he or she owns and its value. The agreement is in writing. Both have a full and fair opportunity to review the agreement and to negotiate its terms. That means that they have enough time to think about it and have their own attorney review it. It won't work to deliver the proposed document to the other partner on the eve of the wedding.

You are probably wondering why this chapter is included in a book on estate planning. It's because the agreement is one of the ways you can clarify what you really intend to have happen to your property when you are gone as well as during your life. The parties agree in advance what each one owns, and what happens to the property if they part or if one dies. A Prenuptial Agreement or a Living Together Agreement defines ownership rights between the two of then, and also to outsiders, including the IRS. They decide how each one's earnings will be treated. Who pays for the new car? What if one charges something and they both use it? Who gets the retirement package? Are they responsible for each other's health care costs (this is a big ticket item for seniors who chose to live together). If he pays for the mortgage and she keeps up the yard, then does she get an ownership interest in the home's appreciation? These are all legitimate questions.

Some scenarios

1. Kelly only knew one thing: She was very much in love! Although her fiancé told her that he had some big financial problems, she didn't think it would impact her much. It was her sweetheart's lawyer who saved her financial life. When he realized the marriage was coming up, he asked the fiancé to arrange a meeting. That was when she heard the grizzly truth about the IRS lien and the lawsuits against him and his

business. The lawyer explained that she had to have a prenuptial agreement stating that each one's earnings were not owned by the other. If she wanted to own a home, it had to be in her name only and he would have to pay rent to her. She needed a completely separate financial life. This was not to protect the husband's assets, but to protect her future earnings from her husband's creditors. She had to get it in writing, before the wedding. It was worth it. After the wedding, when the IRS tried to garnish her salary, the prenuptial agreement was presented and respected. The IRS went away.

2. Amanda was in love with a man who was married. Not that he or his wife wanted to be married to each other! The couple had long ago parted ways, but they had to stay married. The state where they lived was in the midst of a crisis in health insurance, and at age 58, the only way the wife could get any insurance was through a job of her own, or through his job. She had never worked away from home, making a job for her an unrealistic option. So they had a permanent separation, allowing her to take advantage of his health insurance. Amanda had her own insurance taken care of, and said she'd feel guilty if she insisted on marriage, forcing the other woman into a divorce, and creating a situation that provided no insurance for the wife. Instead, moving in together and buying a house together was a realistic option. They trusted each other completely, and doubted that there would be a fight over who owned what, if they parted. The trouble was that each had grown children from their first marriages. If Amanda or her sweetheart died, they didn't want the kids and the survivor fighting over what they owned. Marriage defines ownership, but their arrangement didn't necessarily tell the world what they intended. They opted for a Living Together Agreement, outlining who owned what, and how the home equity should be divided.

3. Marilyn knew her future husband had tax problems when she married him. She bought a printed prenuptial agreement at the stationery store. According to the agreement, all their earnings were separate property. It didn't say anything in the form about real estate.

She sold the house she had owned before the marriage and they moved to another state. Then they decided to buy another house. But the house they wanted was more than her salary could cover alone. So they used her money from her former house (which was separate property money) and used that as a down payment. They took out a mortgage together, took the deed as community property and made the payments together. The IRS moved to foreclose on the house, claiming that he owned equity in it. Marilyn thought this couldn't happen to her because of the prenuptial agreement. When they bought the house together, and she allowed his name to be on the deed, the IRS treated half of the down payment from her separate property as a gift to him. The home mortgage payments came from his income and hers, so he had an equity stake in the house. The IRS wanted the equity in the house to pay his back taxes, and they wanted both his half of the down payment and his half of the gain that had accumulated. After all, it must be his house because his name was on the deed.

Marilyn had intended to have a separate financial life as long as her husband had tax problems, but she didn't follow through when it came to buying the house. She was eventually able to unravel the down payment issue with the IRS, but it was an uphill battle with a lot of expense. She knew the first rule (write and sign the agreement) but she forgot the second rule (live the agreement).

Same Sex Couples

This is a good place to mention the issue of same sex partners. Since marriage is not an option in most states, this group of people can only be given the status of domestic partners. The laws in the states vary on this topic, and if unmarried domestic partners are given any rights in a particular state, they may not flow in the same manner that I described for married people in this chapter. They may be similar, however. Instead of a community property or marital interest argument, there may be something more akin to partnership theory. So the warnings that I have given above apply to same sex partners. If this is an issue for you, be sure you check your state's statutes and caselaw. In this area, as well as others, remember that the agreement is not necessarily about the conflicts between you and your partner. The agreement may be necessary to protect your partner from third parties who would deprive your partner of your intended gifts.

This is a necessary part of the estate plan!

Anybody with a domestic partner, a second marriage or a significant separate estate (previously earned assets or an inheritance) should include an agreement with their beloved as a basic part of the estate plan. You may want your partner to get some of what you own, or you may want your partner to get only a part, or nothing. But it's up to you to get that agreement in writing before you pass on. You don't want your favorite people (children and sweetheart) fighting when you're gone. You definitely don't want a big attorney bill attached to your estate debts. You don't want your dirty laundry displayed in open court. You don't want the uncertainty of a judge deciding how much your partner gets. A prenuptial or living together agreement is a much safer and cheaper way to go.

Chapter 18: Community Property Agreements

Imagine that you are a young woman in New England, madly in love with an ambitious, handsome man in 1850. He wants you to marry him and go out to the wild west, where there is enough land for any man who wants to farm it. There's not just land: there's gold too! It's a dangerous trip and you may not even live through the dangerous terrain. You'll have to say good bye to your family, probably forever. You may not see a city for years. You'll have your first baby on the prairie. You will probably suffer hardship, have no medical care, live near bears, and be just plain lonely. If that handsome ambitious man does well, guess what....you don't own a thing! Any takers? Well, there weren't many. It was hard to get women into the West. That's how community property sprang into life! The Spanish settlers brought it with them from their own country, and it became a lure to bring women to settle the untamed lands.

There are nine community property states.[64] If you live in a community property state, then what you and your partner earn, during the marriage, and while living in the community property state, is community property. No matter which one of you earned it, both of you are entitled to half of it. Inherited property and gifts are not community property. The key is that it must be earned. Anything that doesn't fit into the definition of community property, is separate property.

Each of the states has different rules on the finer details. For instance, suppose you inherited an apartment building. In Washington, the income from the rentals is separate property. In other community property states, that might not be the same result. You must check in the state where you live.

---

[64] They are: Arizona, California, Idaho, Louisiana, New Mexico, Nevada, Texas, Washington, Wisconsin.

If you give your separate property to your spouse, then it's a gift that cannot be taken back. I always advise my clients who are inheriting money to open a separate account, with only their names on it. The person inheriting shouldn't put the spouse's name on the account, unless he/she understands that they are not going to get that money back if the marriage ends. (One man told me, with a big laugh, that his wife of 40 years had put up with him for so long, that she deserved all of it!)

If you've come from a non-community property state, and move into a community property state, you may not realize there is a problem. In the non-community property states, the worker owns everything he or she earns. Those states make it equitable for the non-working spouse by requiring the worker to give a "forced share" of the estate to the surviving spouse. For instance, the husband may own everything, but in his state, he is forced to leave his wife at least 35% of his assets. So the problem arises when the couple leaves New York (where he would have been forced to give her a share), and they move to Washington. In Washington, there is no forced share at death, because everything is community property. But this couple's property isn't owned by the "community" of the two of them. The definition of community property says that it's property earned in the community property state. So the wife can end up without the protection of the forced share from the former home state and without any community property from the new state! Ouch! Some states have a solution called "quasi-community property". It means that if the asset would have been community property in the place where it was earned, then that state will treat it as community property. However, it may not apply to all the assets he owns (such as real estate) and every state may not use quasi-community property theory as a solution to this situation. Moving from one state to another means you must check in with a local lawyer to make sure everybody is safe. Once again, it may not be each other that you are worried about. It may be the kids from the prior marriage.

Community property agreements are written for several reasons. One is to clarify that all property, except inheritances and gifts, are owned by both partners. There's a special opportunity in using the community property agreement. It can be written to say that, at the moment of death, all the property of either one spouse is given immediately to the other. If you have given everything away at the moment of death, then you own nothing. And if you own nothing, then nobody has to file a probate case in the court. The community property agreement is known as "the poor man's Will", because it disposes of property to the spouse in an instant. I don't advise you to rely upon only this document. But if it makes sense for you, then your planner should prepare it.

And this is important: A community property agreement trumps a Will! If there is a conflict between the Will and the community property agreement, the community property agreement wins.

A community property agreement which transfers property at death is not a correct choice for a couple with tax planning needs. And there is another down side to this document: you cannot revoke it unless the spouse agrees. Remember that this is a contract. You may one day feel less agreeable with your spouse and wish that you could end the agreement, but you may not be able to do that. Use this document with eyes wide open!

Chapter 19: **Where Are Your Records?**

Everybody in New Orleans lost their Wills……..

And the deeds to their homes,
Their retirement account numbers
Their social security cards
Their passports and visas
Their birth certificates….

And the list goes on. I've been telling my clients, for several years, that their important documents should be sent away from their locale because we have our own natural disasters, (earthquake, tsunami and volcanic ash). After Hurricane Katrina destroyed so many homes and businesses in New Orleans, it became even more obvious to me that my clients need another nudge to keep family information in a safe place, away from local disaster.

Think what would happen if your home were destroyed in a natural disaster or terrorist attack. It doesn't matter where you live, there's a natural disaster lurking. Like the Katrina victims, you may have to leave on a Red Cross bus, with nothing but your spouse and your children. How would you live? You may have a bank account, but how could you prove who you are? You probably have your driver's license, but I bet you don't have your social security card, or a copy of your bank statement. How would you get access to the money you've put aside? You may try to get government help, and that requires proof of your children's birth. Do you have copies of their birth certificates? Certainly, you didn't bring them with you in an emergency. Your house may be destroyed. Do you know the name of the insurance company that is insuring it?

You've got life insurance, retirement accounts, savings. It's time to make sure that all of those safety nets work. They don't work if the people you love can't get access to them in a time of need. Look at the list of documents and information below. Then promise that you will immediately find a Saturday afternoon to gather up these items, and make copies. If you don't want the bulk, then scan them and put it all onto a compact disk.

Promise that you will get these things delivered to someone you trust with your financial life. That person should be far from where you live. If you're on a coast, send the copies to someone inland. If you're in twister country, send the documents to someone out of the same disaster area. I know this is asking a lot. But it's not asking too much. Take care of this final detail of your family's safety right away. The people in New Orleans had some warning. You will have no warning of an earthquake, terrorist attack, hurricane, or a flash flood. Do it now.[65]

Documents Suggested for Copy

Wills, Powers of Attorney and Health Care Directives
Deeds to Real Estate
Title Insurance
Bank Statement
Retirement Statement
Brokerage Account Statements
Safety Deposit Box information (Bank name, box number, contents)
Passport/Visa
Social Security Cards
One Credit Card
Marriage License
Birth Certificates

---

[65] You can gather this information very efficiently by using "The Family Love Letter" created and copyrighted by attorney John J. Scroggin. You can find a printable form at his web site: www.scrogginlaw.com.

Life Insurance Policies (the entire policy)
Health Insurance Policies
Car Insurance Policy
Homeowners Insurance Policy
Umbrella Insurance Policy
Debt owed you to by others (promissory notes)
Photos of personal items that you have insured
Pet information
A personal statement of your health: This one takes time and attention
    A short statement of your health history
    Allergies (including medicine allergies)
    Medications
    Surgeries
    Current physicians
Things that would identify you and your family: Scars, dental work, tattoos (Sorry! This one is gruesome, but necessary)

Afterward

No matter your situation, you really need to have the fine points of the law applied to your particular situation. There is no substitute for competent estate planning. If I've persuaded you of only one thing, remember at least that! And remember that this is not a do it yourself book!

The next most important thing to say is that you really must stay educated on the topic of estate planning. Even if you hire the best planner in the world today, it doesn't do you much good if the law changes and your documents don't change with it. Keep in touch with your advisor.

Best wishes!

Madeline Gauthier
Attorney at Law
Bellevue, WA, 2006